How to Use this Book

LIST EIGHT THINGS - That you want to learn about:

1.
2.
3.
4.
5.
6.
7.
8.

Action Steps:

1. Go to the library or bookstore.
2. Bring home a stack of at least eight interesting books and movies about these topics. Choose some books that have diagrams, instructions and illustrations.

Supplies Needed:

You will need pencils, colored pencils, pens and markers. If learning from YouTube you need internet and a viewing device.

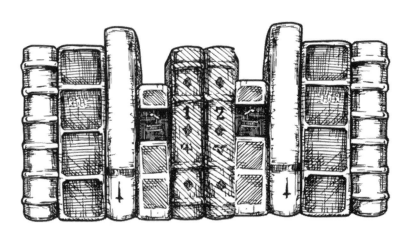

Choose EIGHT Books To Use As School Books!

1. Write down the titles on each cover below.
2. Keep your stack of books in a safe place.
3. Be ready to read your books for at least 1 hour per day.
4. Complete 5 – 8 pages each day in this workbook.

This page is for other books that you may use.

1. Write down the titles on each cover below.
2. Keep your stack of books in a safe place.
3. If you finish reading a book, or do not like one of your books, just get a new one.

Write down an inspirational quote:

To-Do List

Nature Study

Go outside and make a realistic drawing of something you find in in nature.

Reading Time - 1 Hour

Choose Four Books - Read from each book for 15 minutes.
Copy a sentence or picture from each book here:

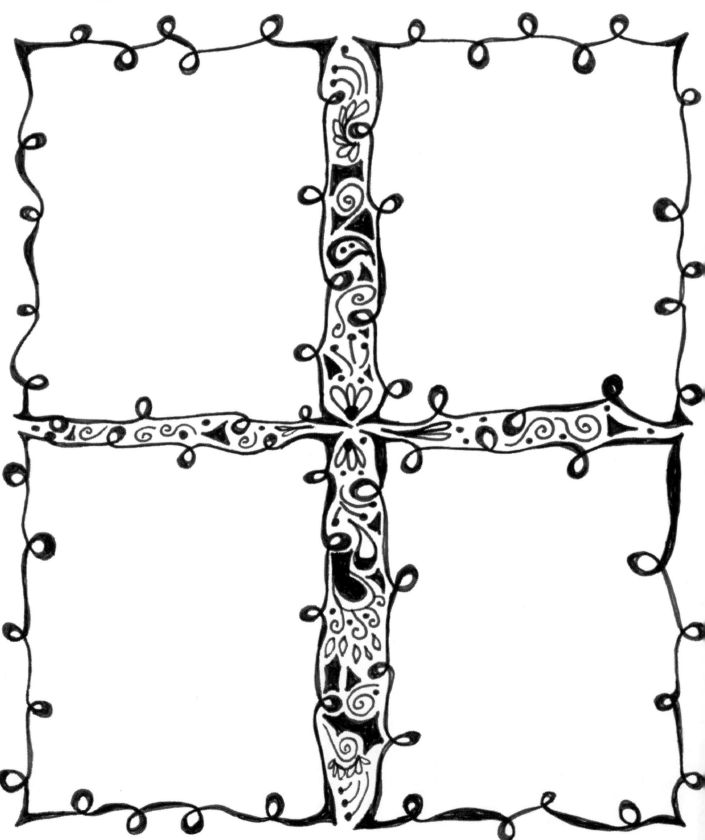

Copywork

Find an interesting paragraph in one of your books and copy it. Be diligent to make your writing look exactly like it does the book.

TITLE:_____

Page Number:_____

Emotions & Moods

How are your feeling today? Color the facial expressions to match today's moods.

Can you of three things that might help your mood improve?
1.
2.
3.

Listening Time

Listen to an audio book or classical music or ask someone to read a story to you while you color and draw on the next page.

What are you listening to?

_____

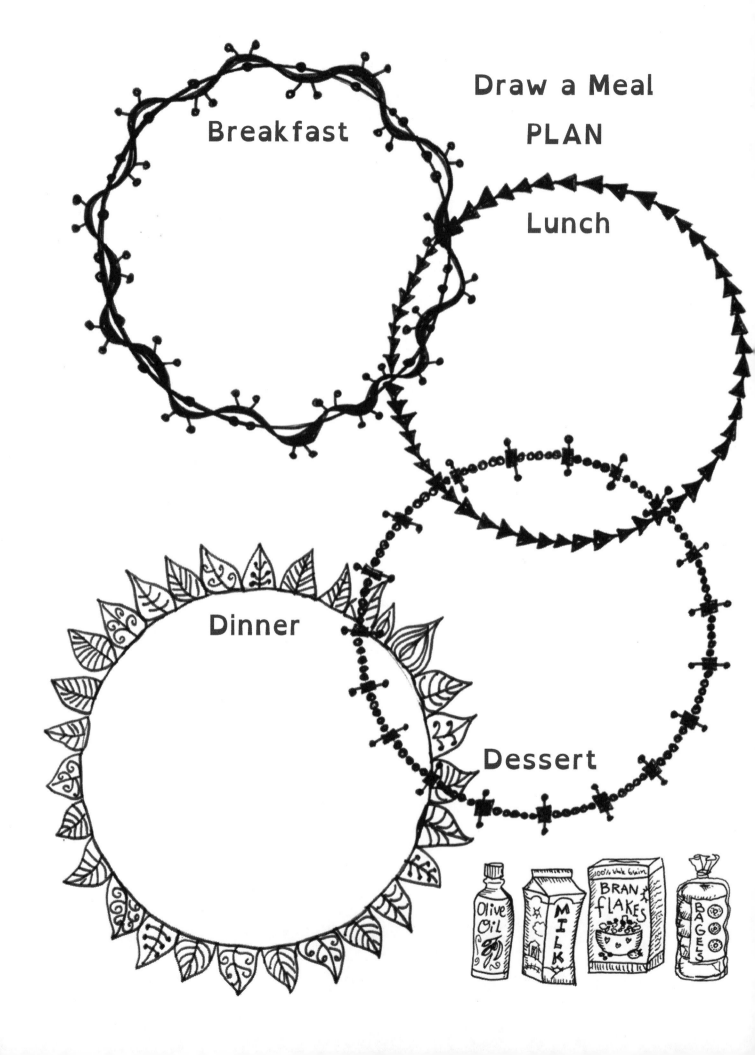

Recipe:

_____

Serves:

Prep Time:

Ingredients:

Instructions:

Shopping List:

Reading Time - 1 Hour
Choose Four Books - Read from each book for 15 minutes.
Copy a sentence or picture from each book here:

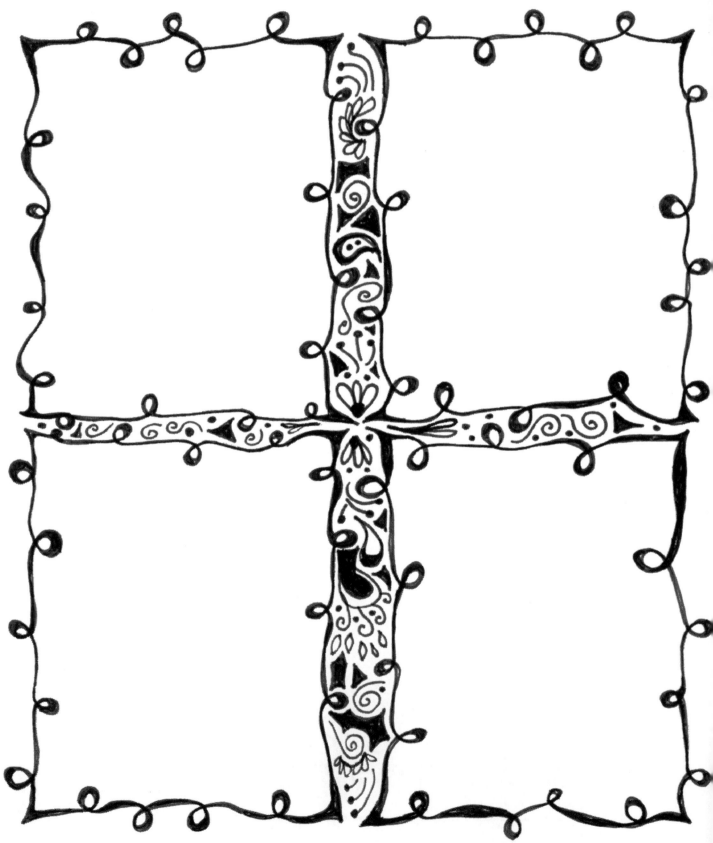

Copywork

Find an interesting paragraph in one of your books and copy it. Be diligent to make your writing look exactly like it does the book.

TITLE:_____

Page Number:_____

_____
_____
_____
_____
_____
_____
_____
_____
_____
_____
_____

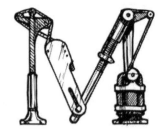

Math Practice

You can design something. You can make graphs, maps, or geometric designs. You can practice math problems.

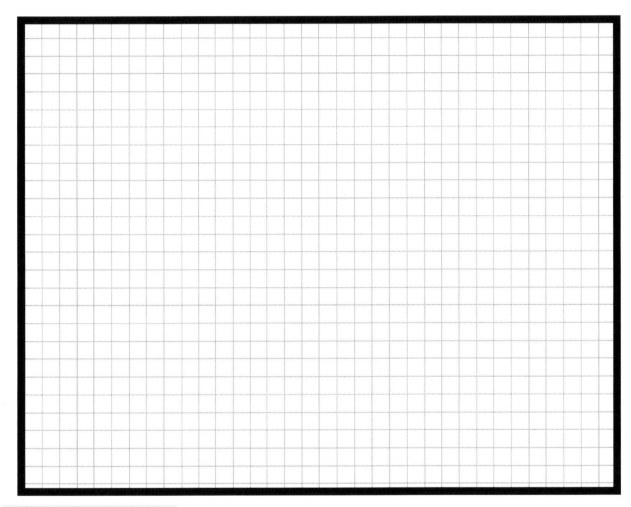

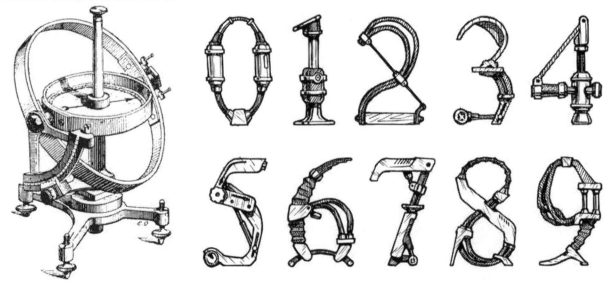

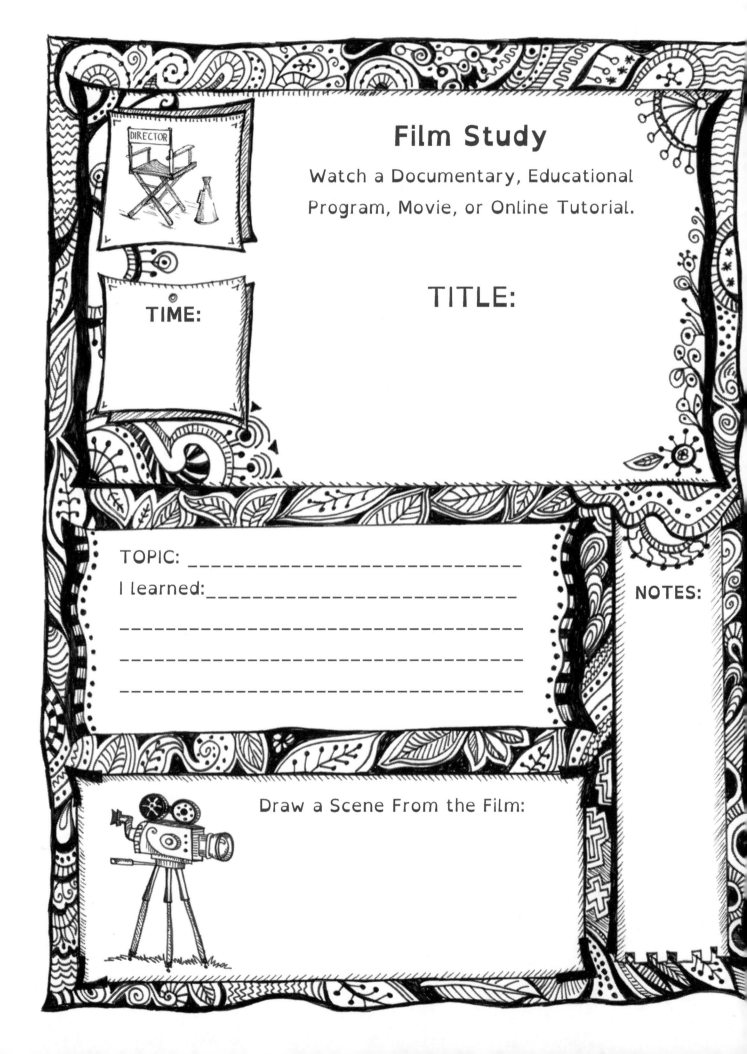

Spelling Time

Find 20 Words with **6** letters each.
Look in your books for words.
Write the words here:

Object Lesson

Look at this interesting object from the past.
Do you know what it is?

_____

What could it be used for?

_____
_____

How would the world be different
if this was not invented?

_____
_____
_____
_____
_____
_____
_____
_____
_____

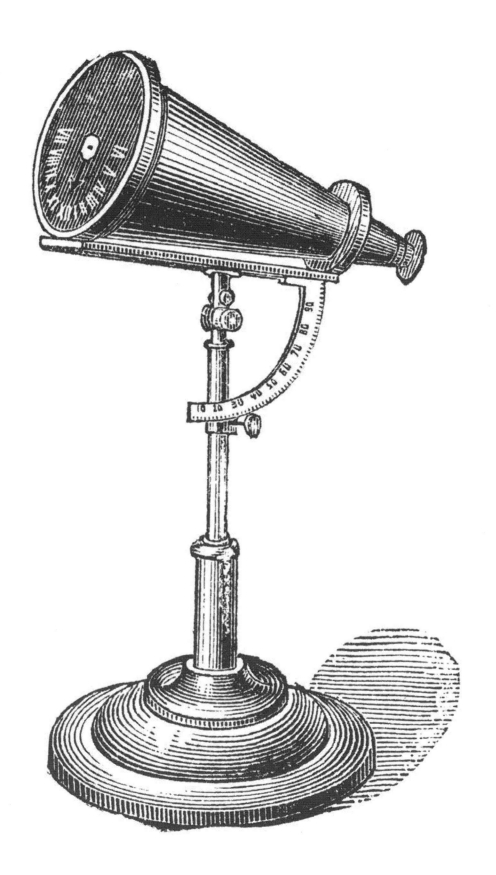

Write down an inspirational quote:

To-Do List

Nature Study

Go outside and make a realistic drawing of something you find in in nature.

Reading Time - 1 Hour
Choose Four Books - Read from each book for 15 minutes.
Copy a sentence or picture from each book here:

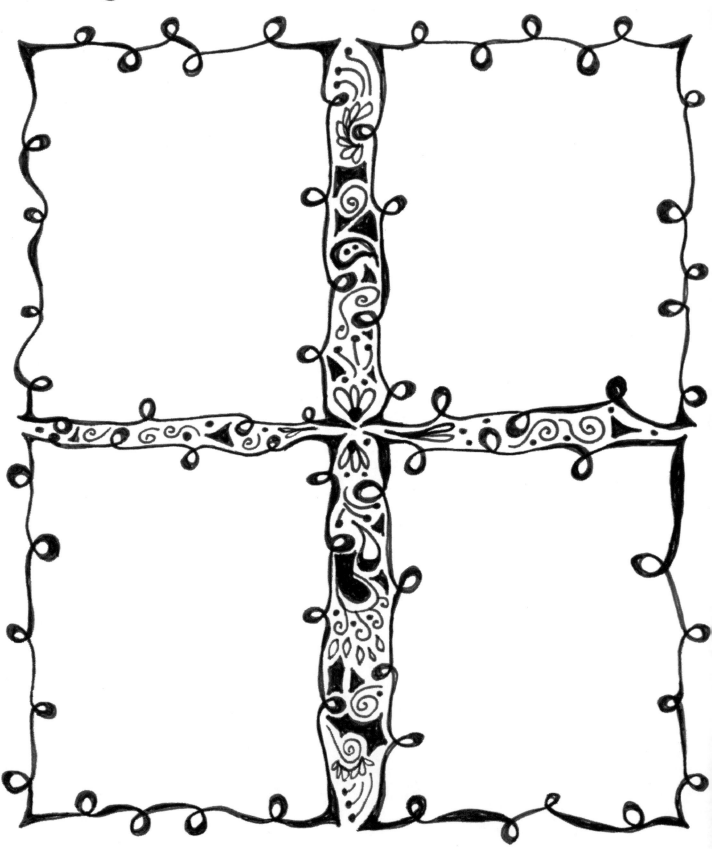

Copywork

Find an interesting paragraph in one of your books and copy it. Be diligent to make your writing look exactly like it does the book.

TITLE:_____

Page Number:_____

Emotions & Moods

How are your feeling today?
Color the facial expressions
to match today's moods.

Can you of three things that might help your mood improve?
1.
2.
3.

Draw Anything

Listening Time

Listen to an audio book or classical music or ask someone to read a story to you while you color and draw on the next page.

What are you listening to?

_____

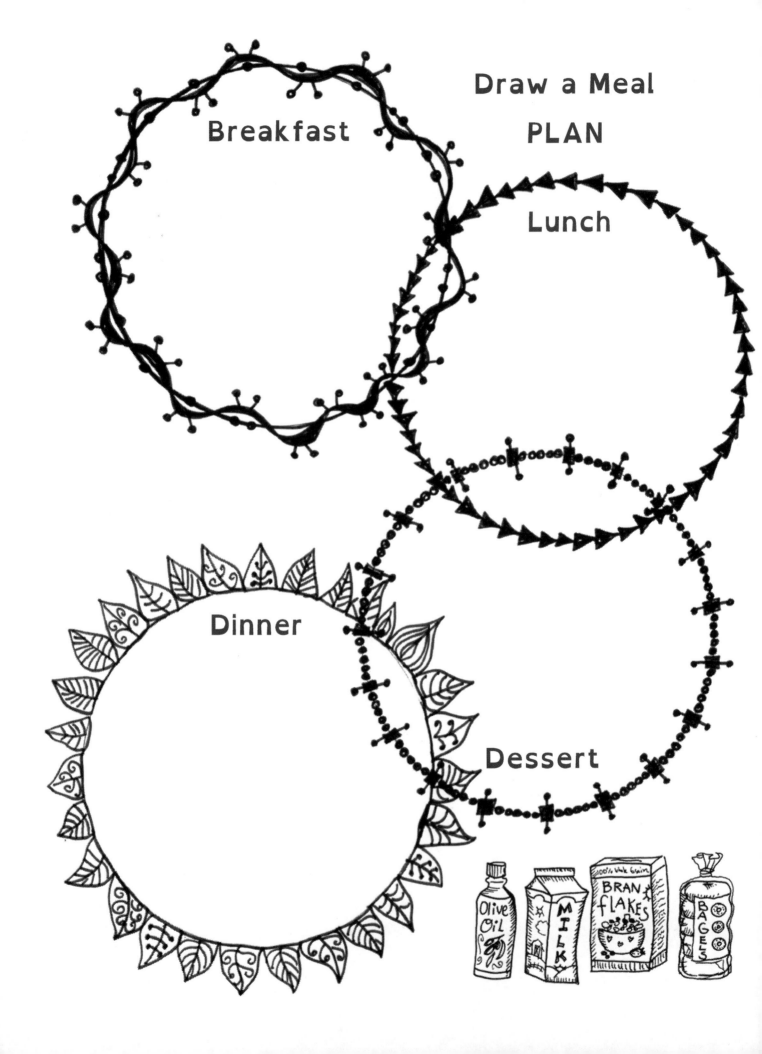

Recipe:

_____

Serves:

Prep Time:

Ingredients:

Instructions:

Shopping List:

Reading Time - 1 Hour

Choose Four Books - Read from each book for 15 minutes.
Copy a sentence or picture from each book here:

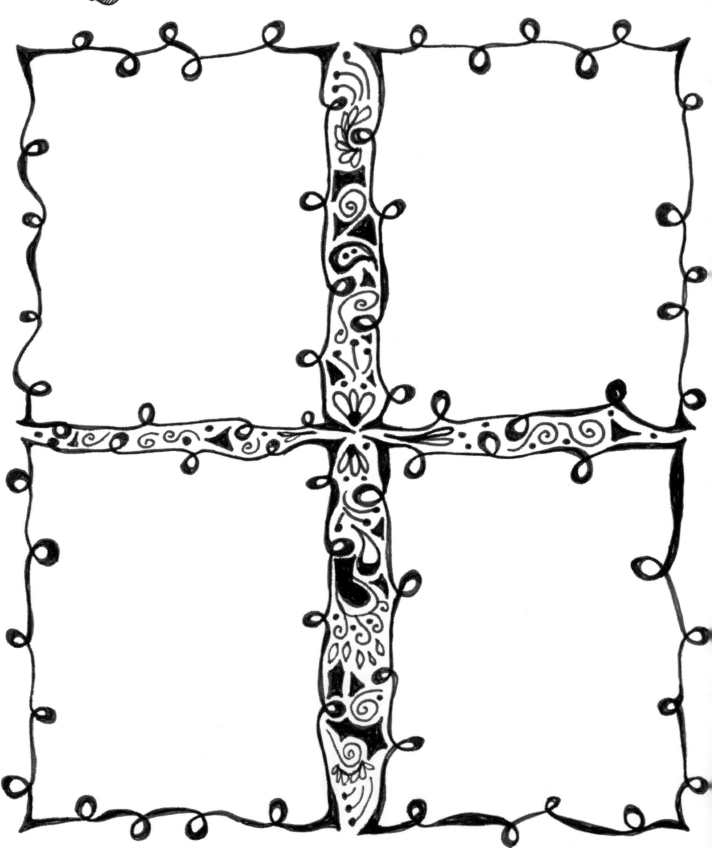

Copywork

Find an interesting paragraph in one of your books and copy it. Be diligent to make your writing look exactly like it does the book.

TITLE:_____

Page Number:_____

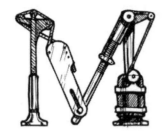

Math Practice

You can design something. You can make graphs, maps, or geometric designs. You can practice math problems.

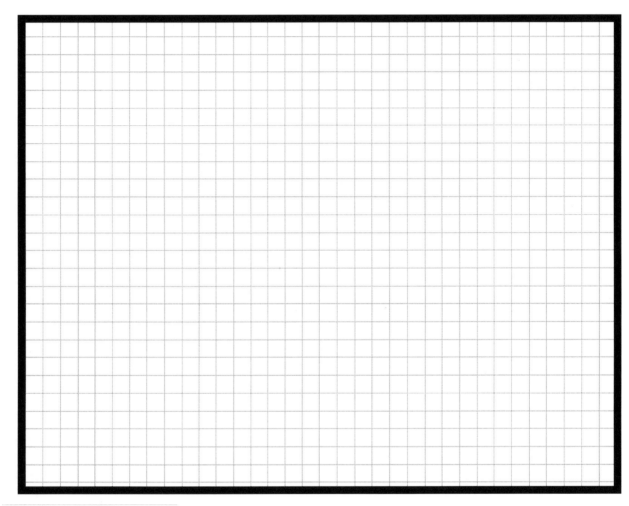

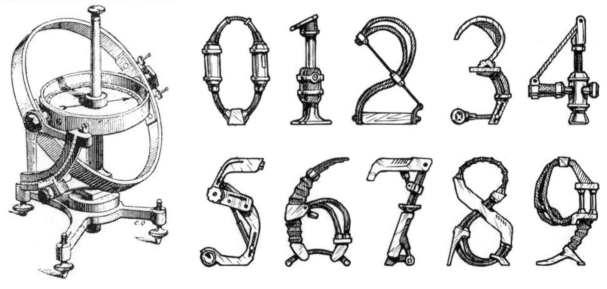

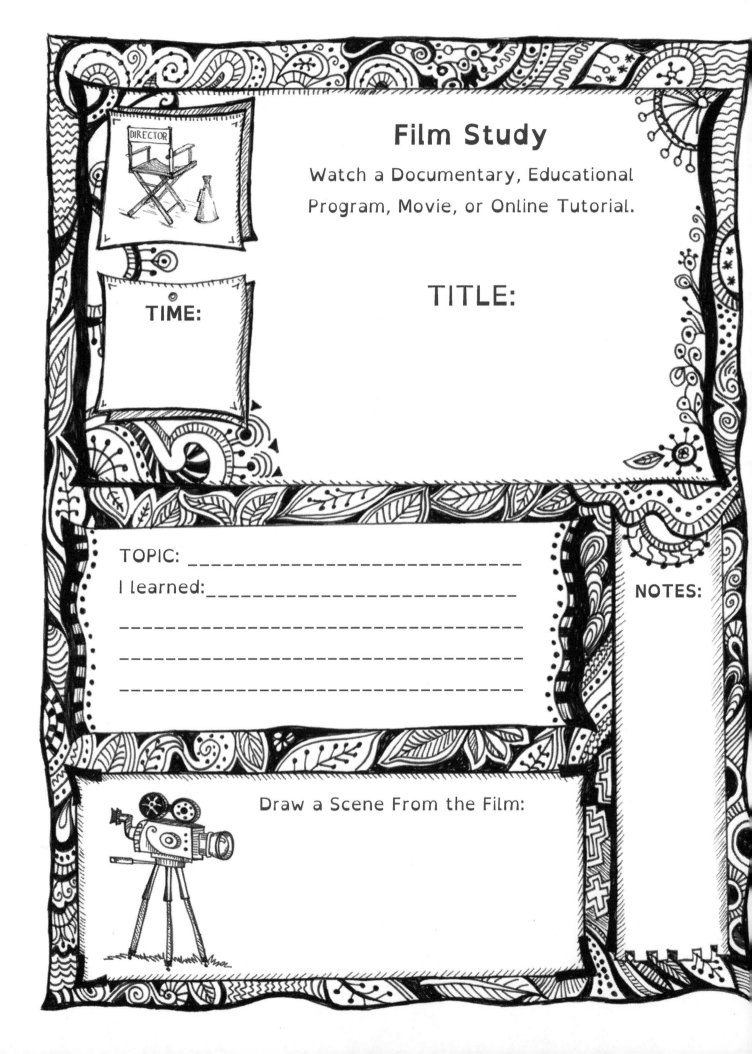

Spelling Time

Find 20 Words with ____ letters each.
Look in your books for words.
Write the words here:

Object Lesson

Look at this interesting object from the past.
Do you know what it is?

_____

What could it be used for?
_____
_____

How would the world be different
if this was not invented?

_____
_____
_____
_____
_____
_____
_____
_____
_____
_____

World News Today!

1. Talk with your family about current events.
2. Look at a newspaper, news broadcast or news website.
3. What do you think is the most important thing that happened in the world today or yesterday?
_____
_____
4. Color the part of the map where the event happened.

5. Draw a picture of the event:

Write down an inspirational quote:

To-Do List

Nature Study

Go outside and make a realistic drawing of something you find in in nature.

Reading Time - 1 Hour

Choose Four Books - Read from each book for 15 minutes.
Copy a sentence or picture from each book here:

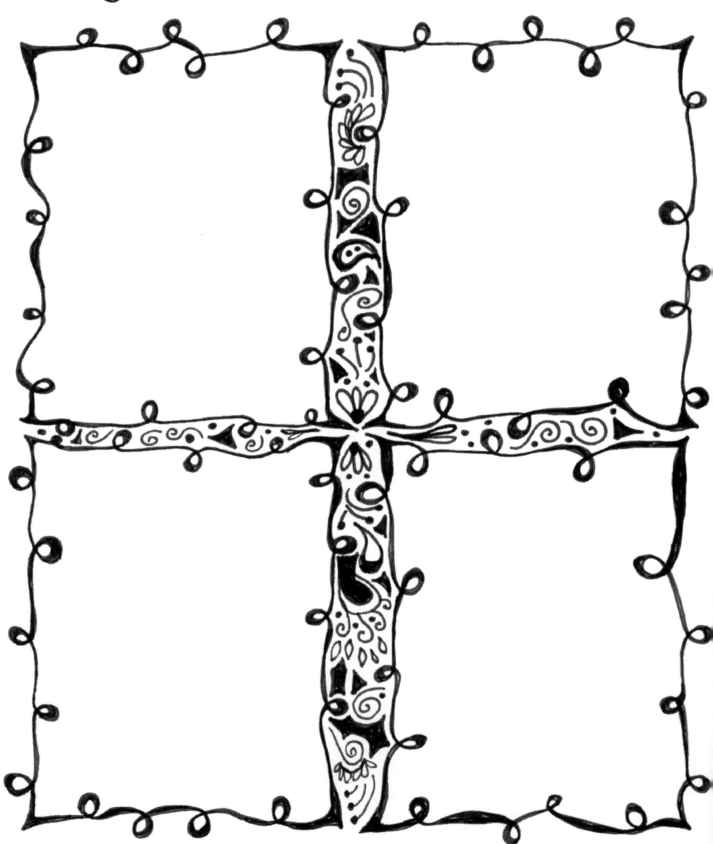

Copywork

Find an interesting paragraph in one of your books and copy it. Be diligent to make your writing look exactly like it does the book.

TITLE:_____

Page Number:_____

_____
_____
_____
_____
_____
_____
_____
_____
_____
_____
_____

Emotions & Moods

How are your feeling today? Color the facial expressions to match today's moods.

Can you of three things that might help your mood improve?

1.
2.
3.

Listening Time

Listen to an audio book or classical music or ask someone to read a story to you while you color and draw on the next page.

What are you listening to?

_____

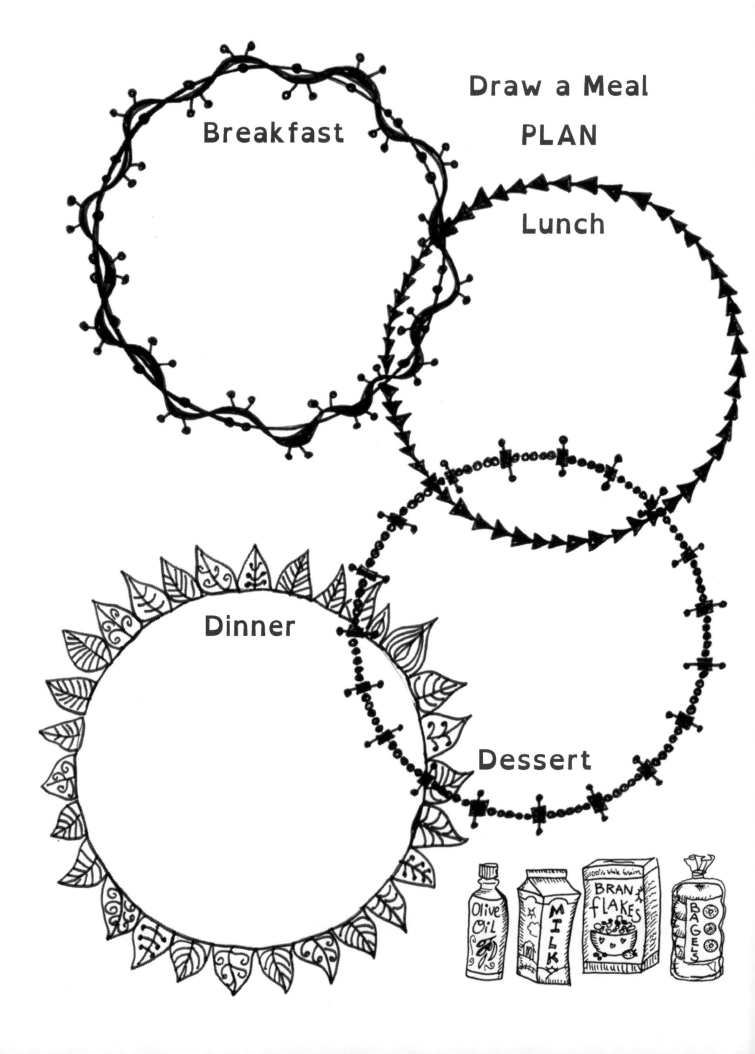

Recipe:

_____

Serves:

Prep Time:

Ingredients:

Instructions:

Shopping List:

Reading Time - 1 Hour

Choose Four Books - Read from each book for 15 minutes.
Copy a sentence or picture from each book here:

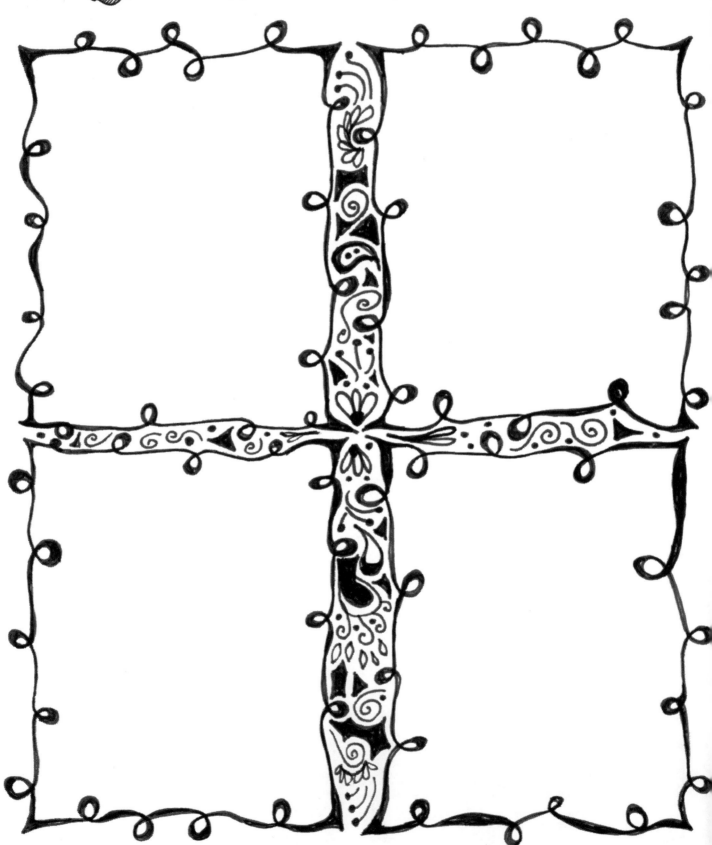

Copywork

Find an interesting paragraph in one of your books and copy it. Be diligent to make your writing look exactly like it does the book.

TITLE:_____

Page Number:_____

_____
_____
_____
_____
_____
_____
_____
_____
_____
_____
_____

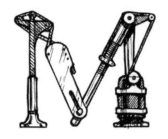

Math Practice

You can design something. You can make graphs, maps, or geometric designs. You can practice math problems.

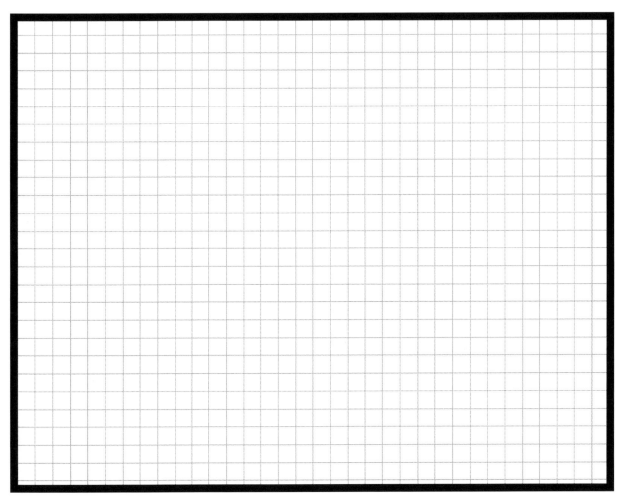

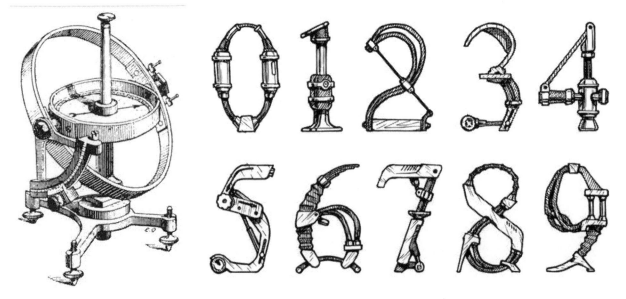

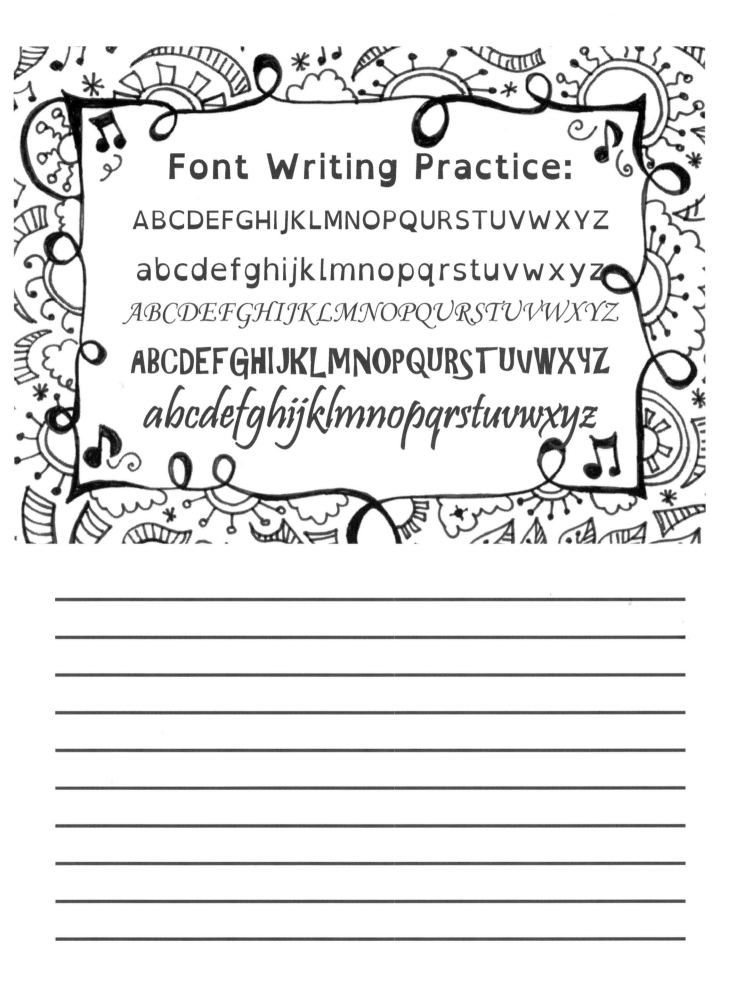

Font Writing Practice:

ABCDEFGHIJKLMNOPQURSTUVWXYZ

abcdefghijklmnopqrstuvwxyz

ABCDEFGHIJKLMNOPQURSTUVWXYZ

ABCDEFGHIJKLMNOPQURSTUVWXYZ

abcdefghijklmnopqrstuvwxyz

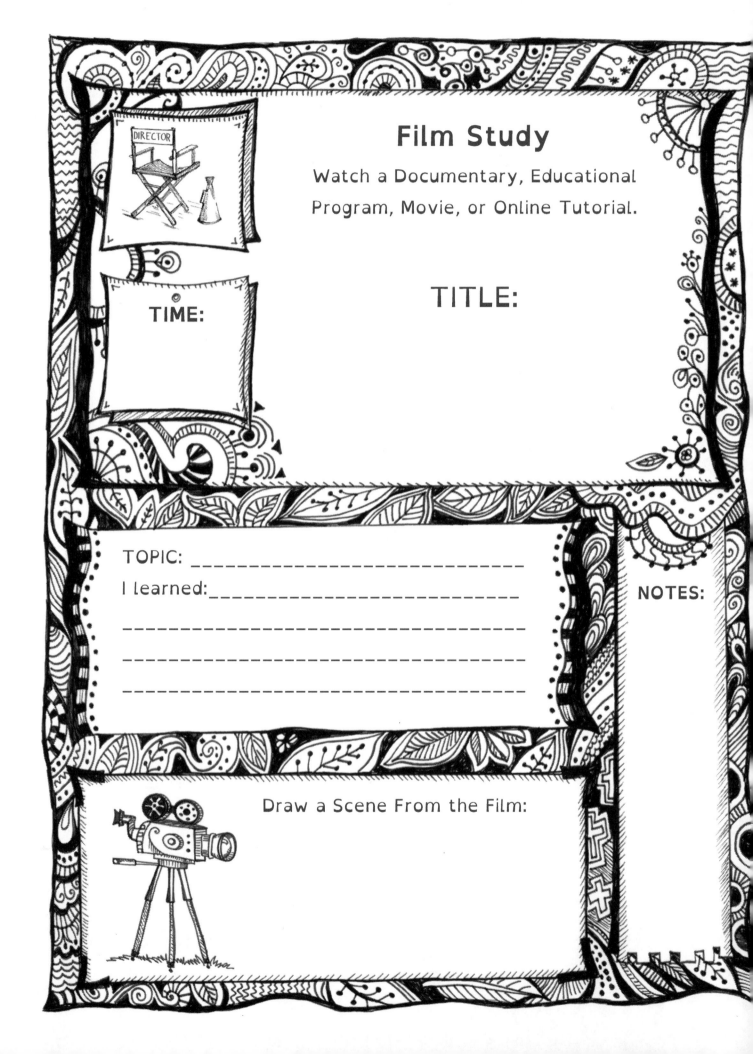

Film Study

Watch a Documentary, Educational Program, Movie, or Online Tutorial.

TIME:

TITLE:

TOPIC: _____
I learned: _____
_____
_____
_____

NOTES:

Draw a Scene From the Film:

Object Lesson

Look at this interesting object from the past.
Do you know what it is?

_____

What could it be used for?

_____
_____

How would the world be different
if this was not invented?

_____
_____
_____
_____
_____
_____
_____
_____

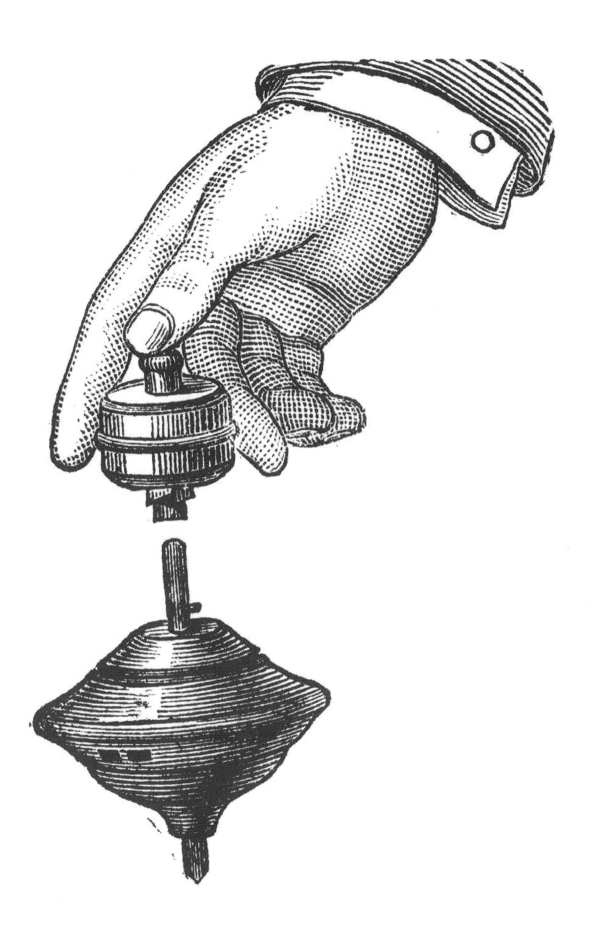

Reading Time - 1 Hour
Choose Four Books - Read from each book for 15 minutes.
Copy a sentence or picture from each book here:

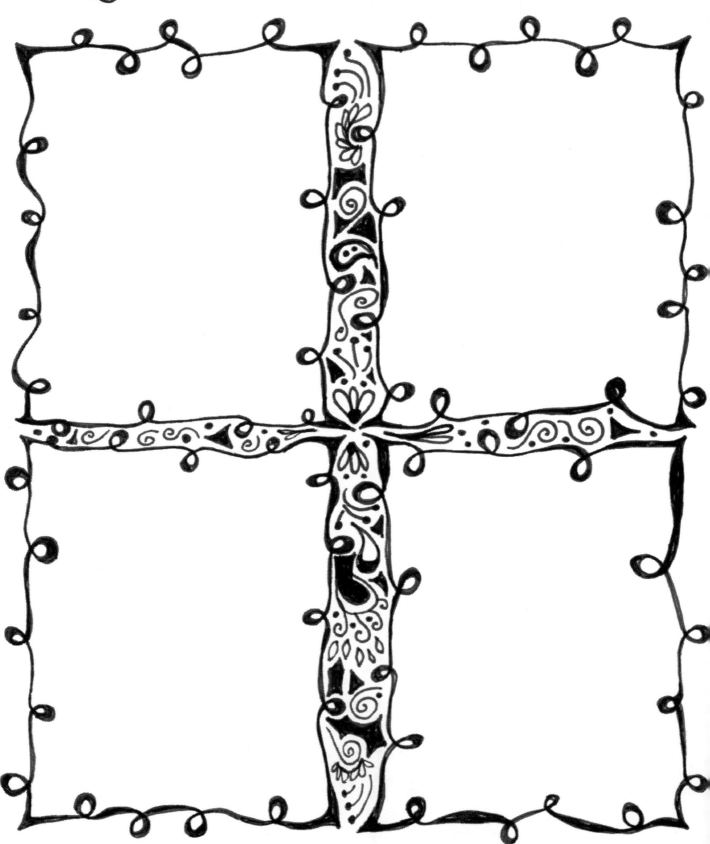

Write down an inspirational quote:

To-Do List
_____
_____
_____
_____
_____
_____

Nature Study

Go outside and make a realistic drawing of something you find in in nature.

Reading Time - 1 Hour
Choose Four Books - Read from each book for 15 minutes.
Copy a sentence or picture from each book here:

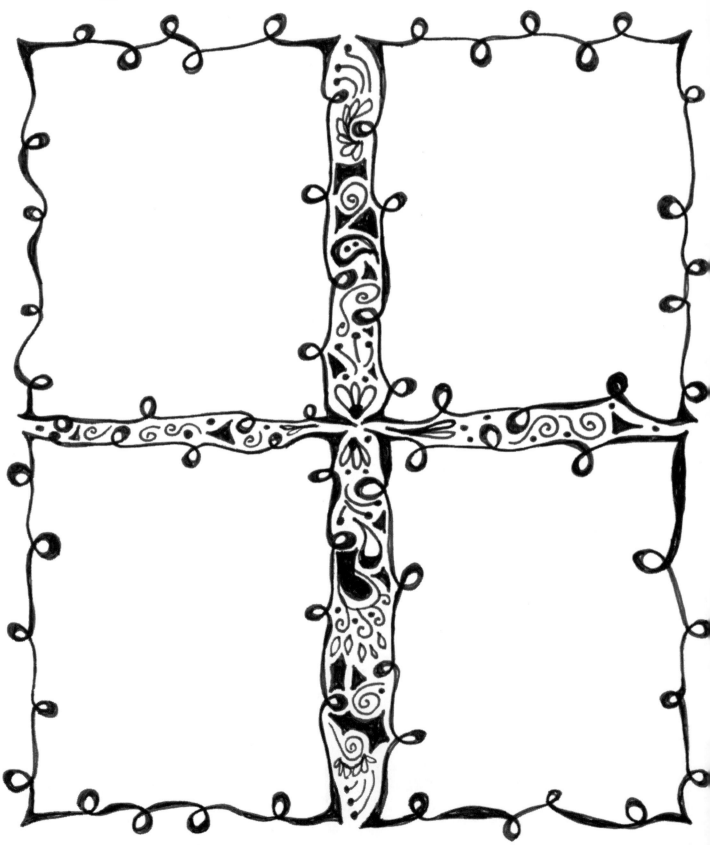

Copywork

Find an interesting paragraph in one of your books and copy it. Be diligent to make your writing look exactly like it does the book.

TITLE:_____

Page Number:_____

Emotions & Moods

How are your feeling today? Color the facial expressions to match today's moods.

Can you of three things that might help your mood improve?
1.
2.
3.

Listening Time

Listen to an audio book or classical music or ask someone to read a story to you while you color and draw on the next page.

What are you listening to?

_____

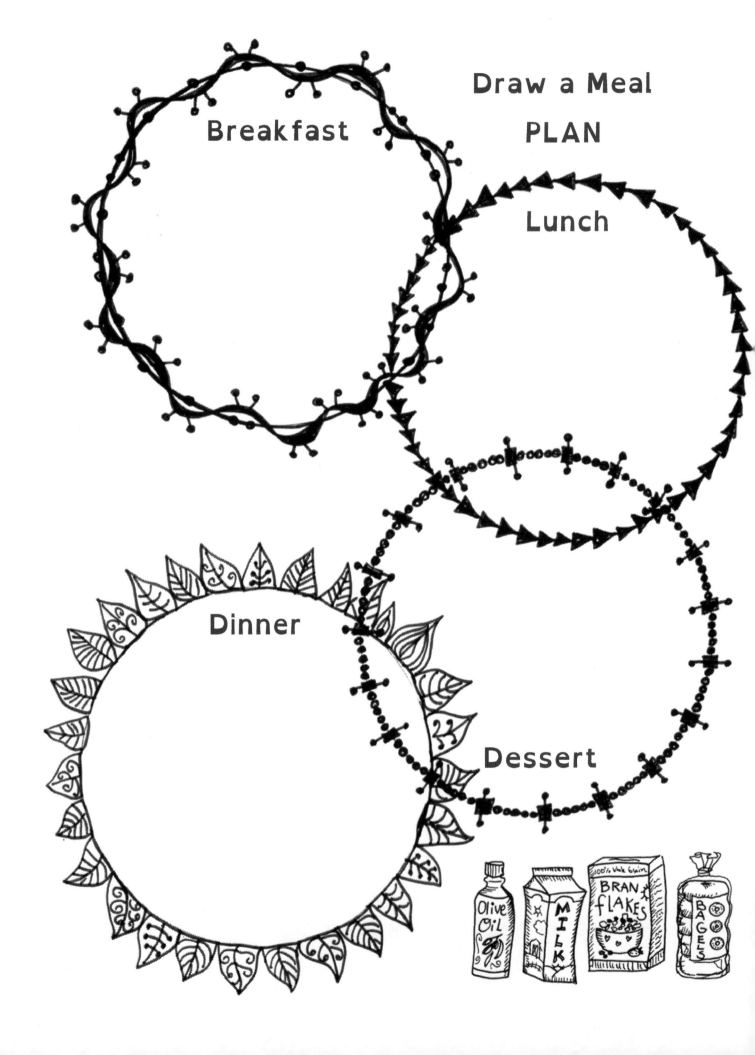

Recipe:

_____

Serves:

Prep Time:

Ingredients:

Instructions:

Shopping List:

Reading Time - 1 Hour
Choose Four Books - Read from each book for 15 minutes.
Copy a sentence or picture from each book here:

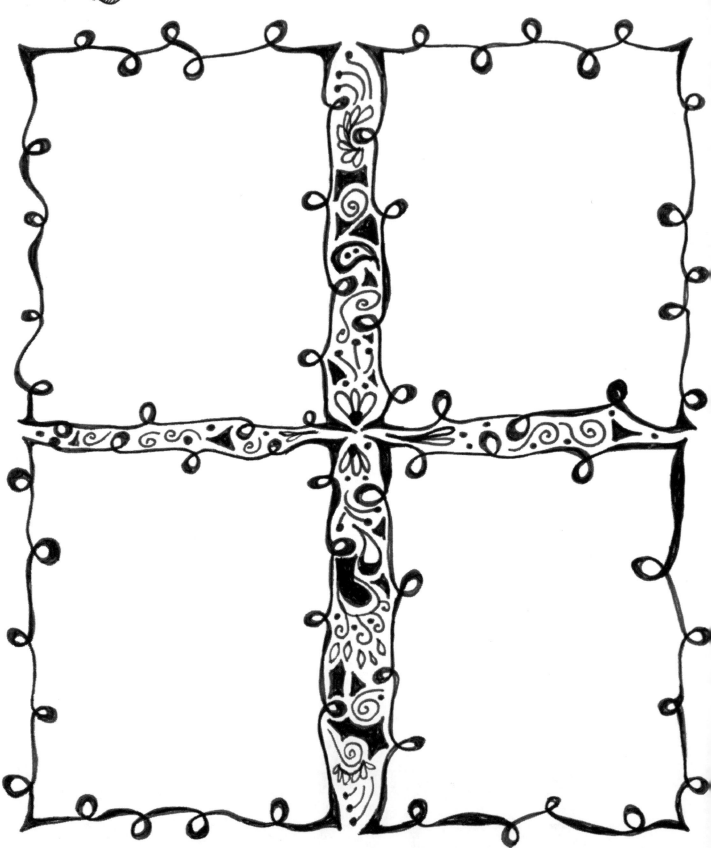

Copywork

Find an interesting paragraph in one of your books and copy it. Be diligent to make your writing look exactly like it does the book.

TITLE:_____

Page Number:_____

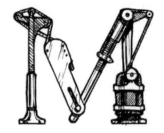

Math Practice

You can design something. You can make graphs, maps, or geometric designs. You can practice math problems.

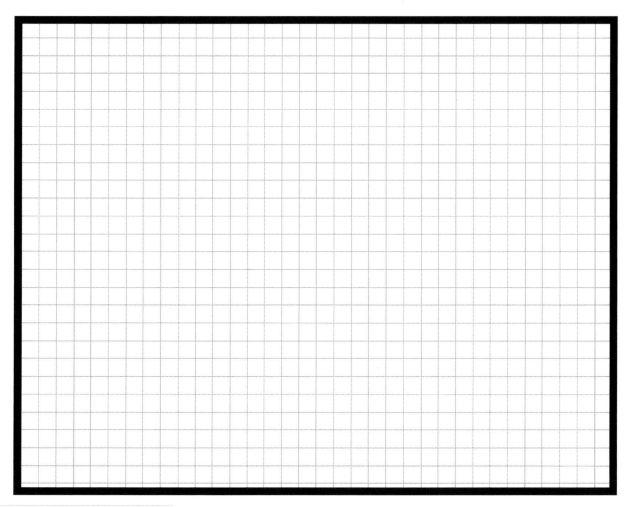

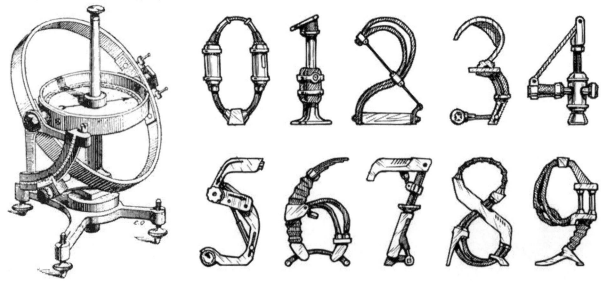

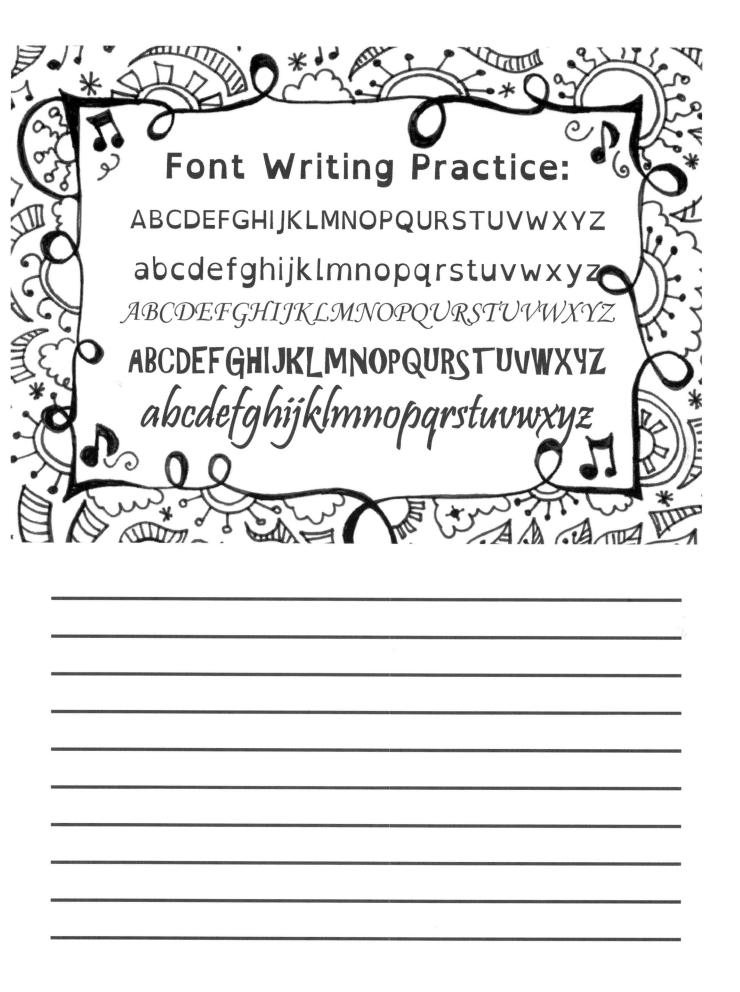

Font Writing Practice:

ABCDEFGHIJKLMNOPQURSTUVWXYZ

abcdefghijklmnopqrstuvwxyz

ABCDEFGHIJKLMNOPQURSTUVWXYZ

ABCDEFGHIJKLMNOPQURSTUVWXYZ

abcdefghijklmnopqrstuvwxyz

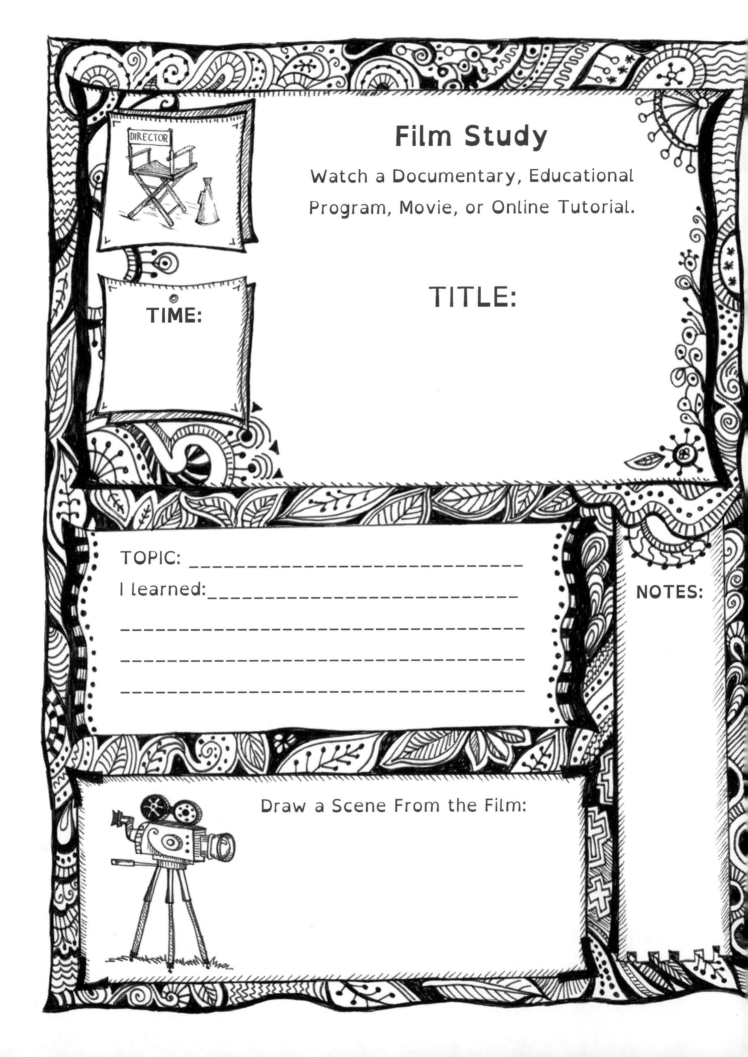

Spelling Time

Find 20 Words with 6 letters each.
Look in your books for words.
Write the words here:

Object Lesson

Look at this interesting object from the past.
Do you know what it is?

_____

What could it be used for?

_____
_____

How would the world be different
if this was not invented?

_____
_____
_____
_____
_____
_____
_____
_____
_____

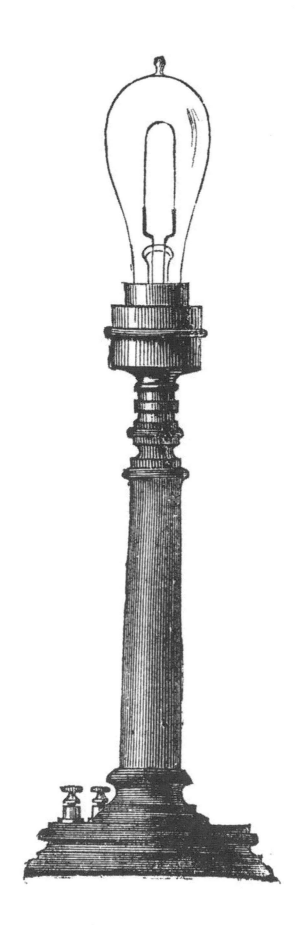

Write down an inspirational quote:

To-Do List
_____
_____
_____
_____
_____
_____

Reading Time - 1 Hour
Choose Four Books - Read from each book for 15 minutes.
Copy a sentence or picture from each book here:

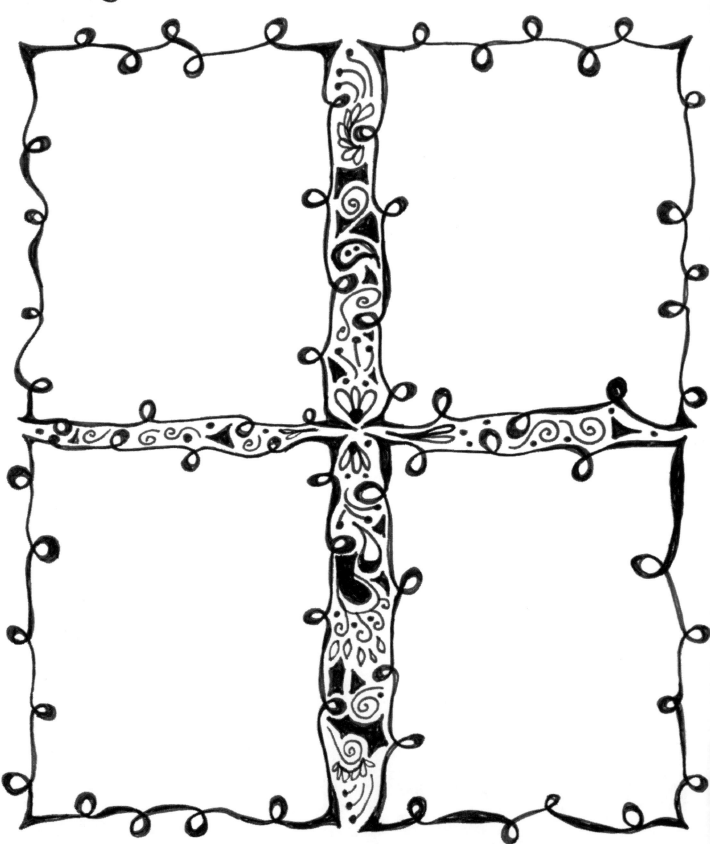

Copywork

Find an interesting paragraph in one of your books and copy it. Be diligent to make your writing look exactly like it does the book.

TITLE:_____

Page Number:_____

_____
_____
_____
_____
_____
_____
_____
_____
_____
_____
_____

Emotions & Moods

How are your feeling today? Color the facial expressions to match today's moods.

Can you of three things that might help your mood improve?
1.
2.
3.

Draw Anything

Listening Time

Listen to an audio book or classical music or ask someone to read a story to you while you color and draw on the next page.

What are you listening to?

_____

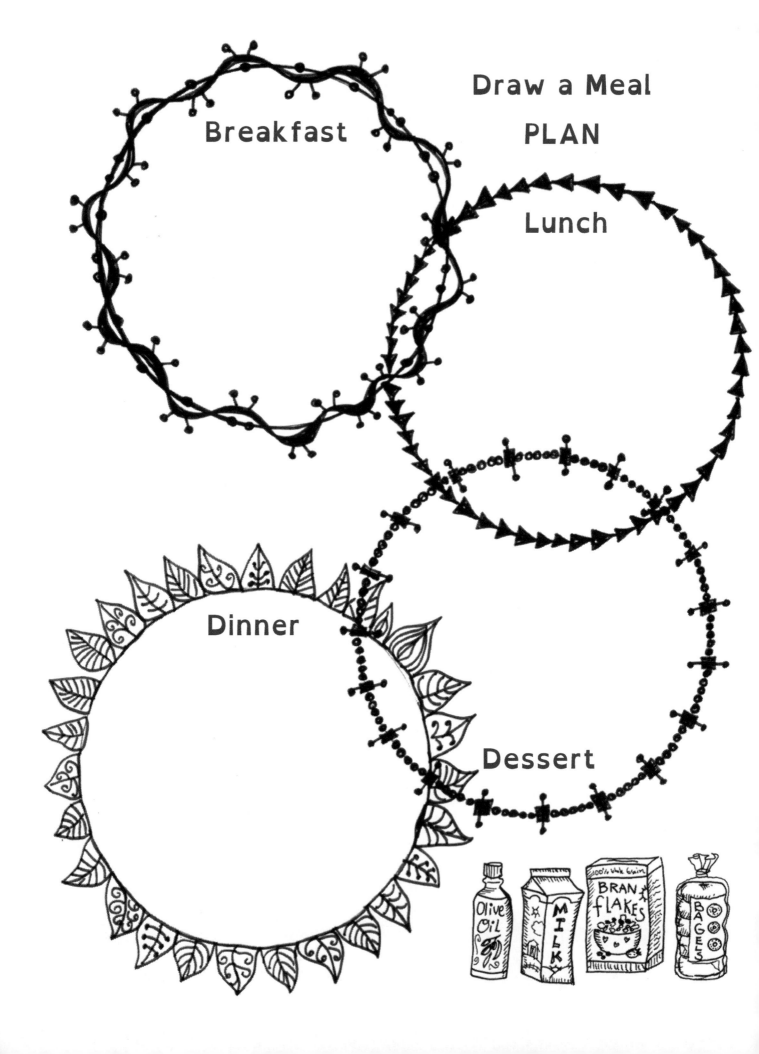

Recipe:

_____

Serves:

Prep Time:

Ingredients:

Instructions:

Shopping List:

Reading Time - 1 Hour

Choose Four Books - Read from each book for 15 minutes.
Copy a sentence or picture from each book here:

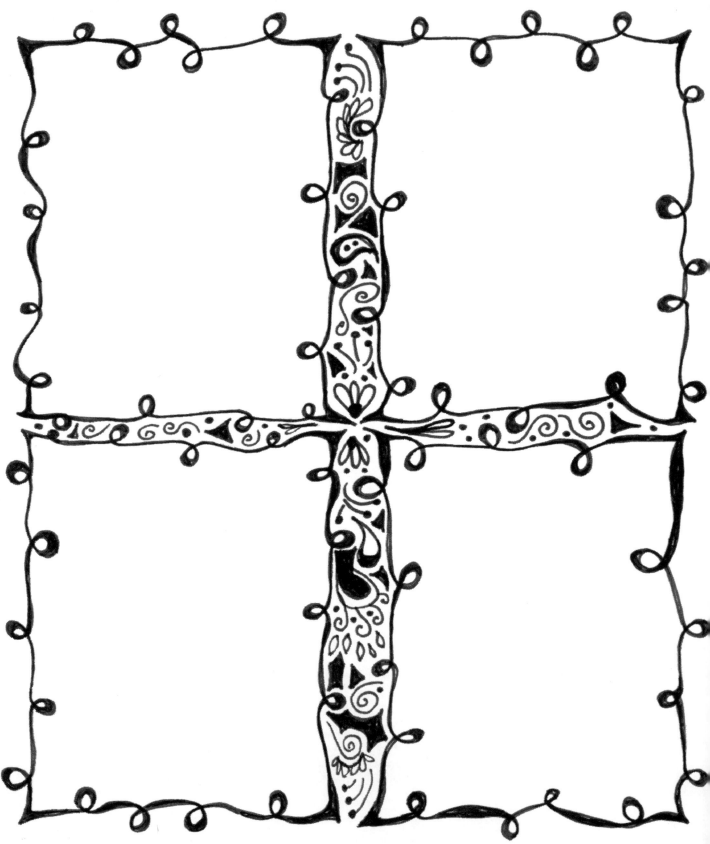

Copywork

Find an interesting paragraph in one of your books and copy it. Be diligent to make your writing look exactly like it does the book.

TITLE:_____

Page Number:_____

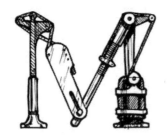

Math Practice

You can design something. You can make graphs, maps, or geometric designs. You can practice math problems.

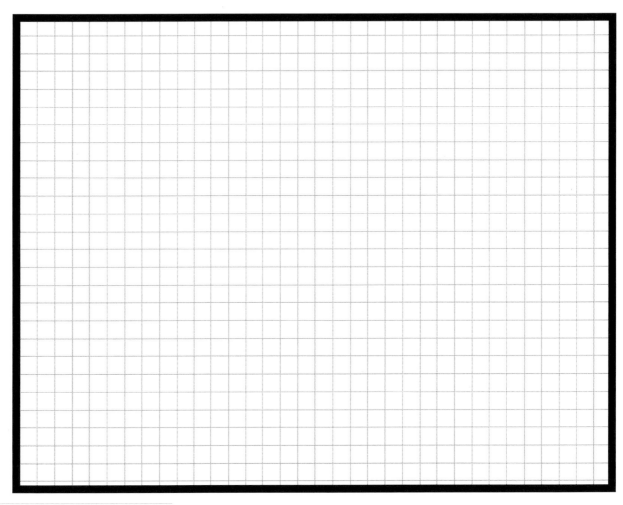

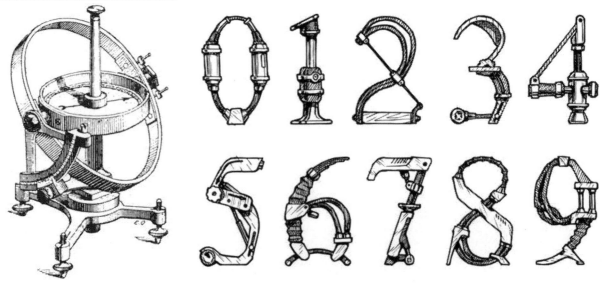

Font Writing Practice:

ABCDEFGHIJKLMNOPQRSTUVWXYZ

abcdefghijklmnopqrstuvwxyz

ABCDEFGHIJKLMNOPQRSTUVWXYZ

ABCDEFGHIJKLMNOPQRSTUVWXYZ

abcdefghijklmnopqrstuvwxyz

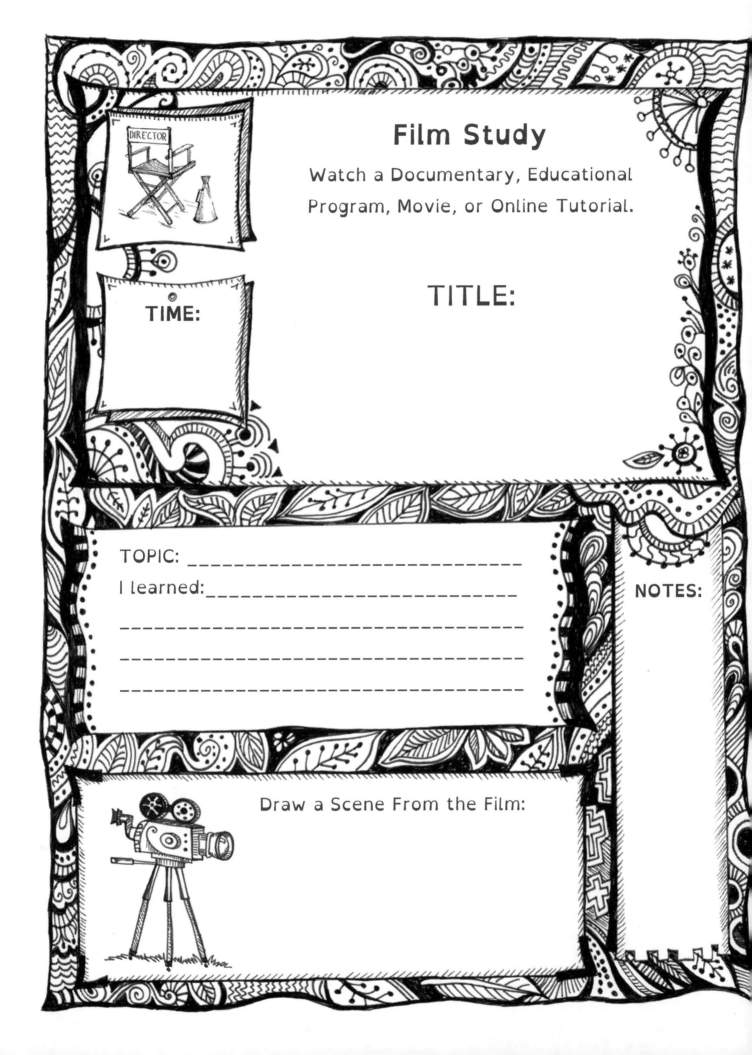

Spelling Time

Find 20 Words with 9 letters each.
Look in your books for words.
Write the words here:

Object Lesson

Look at this interesting object from the past.
Do you know what it is?

_____

What could it be used for?

_____
_____

How would the world be different
if this was not invented?

_____
_____
_____
_____
_____
_____
_____
_____
_____
_____

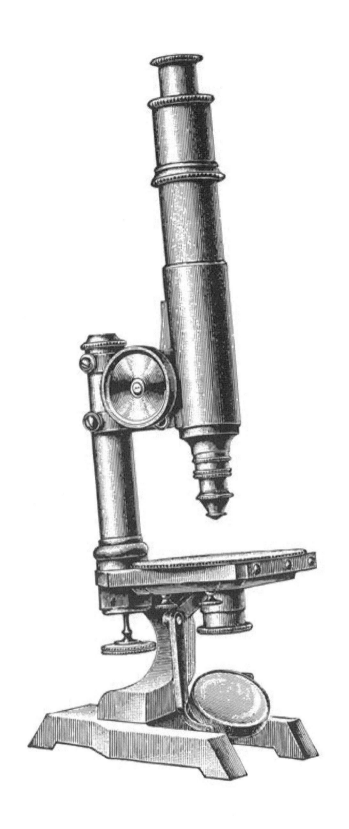

Write down an inspirational quote:

To-Do List

Nature Study

Go outside and make a realistic drawing of something you find in in nature.

Reading Time - 1 Hour

Choose Four Books - Read from each book for 15 minutes.
Copy a sentence or picture from each book here:

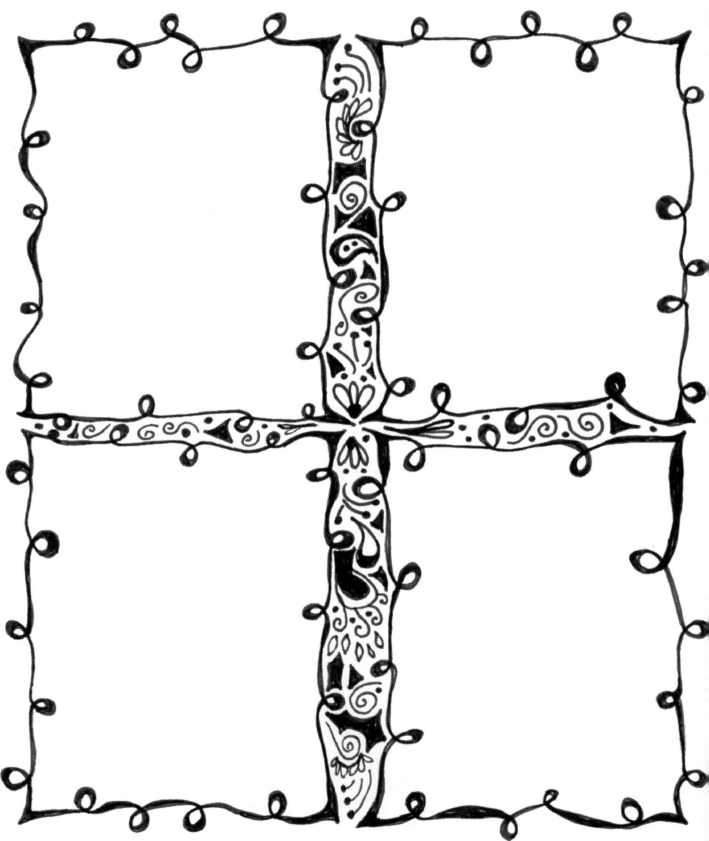

Copywork

Find an interesting paragraph in one of your books and copy it. Be diligent to make your writing look exactly like it does the book.

TITLE:_____

Page Number:_____

Emotions & Moods

How are your feeling today? Color the facial expressions to match today's moods.

Can you of three things that might help your mood improve?
1.
2.
3.

Listening Time

Listen to an audio book or classical music or ask someone to read a story to you while you color and draw on the next page.

What are you listening to?

_____

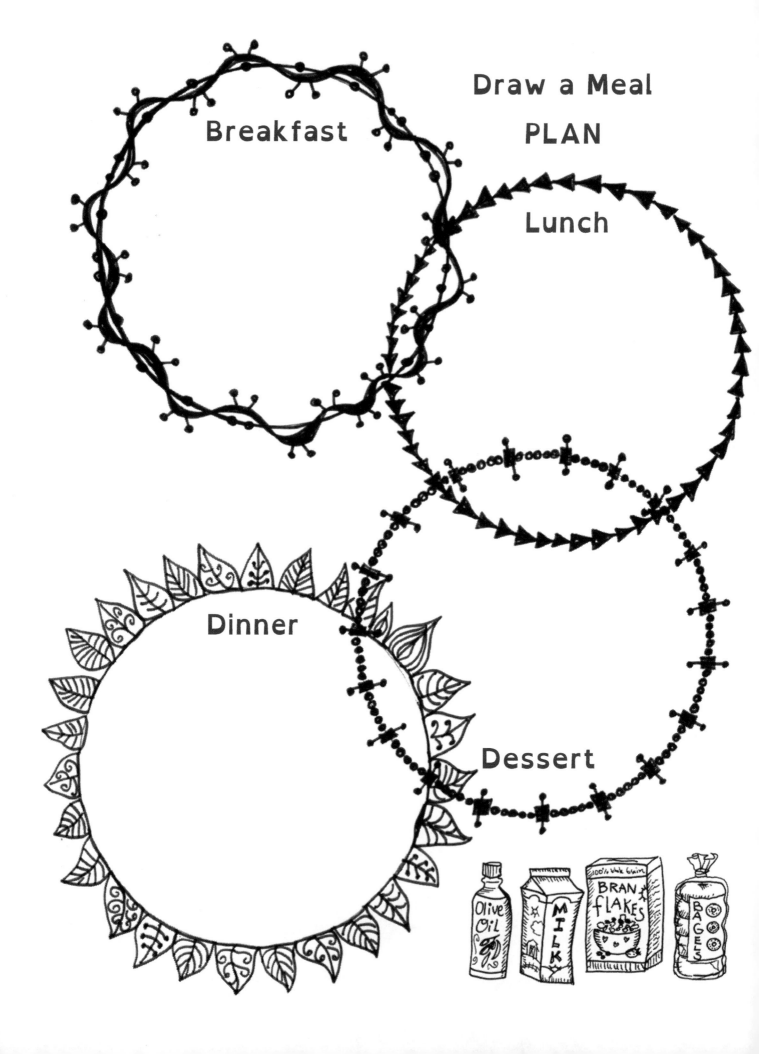

Recipe:

_____

Serves:

Prep Time:

Ingredients:

Instructions:

Shopping List:

Reading Time - 1 Hour

Choose Four Books - Read from each book for 15 minutes.
Copy a sentence or picture from each book here:

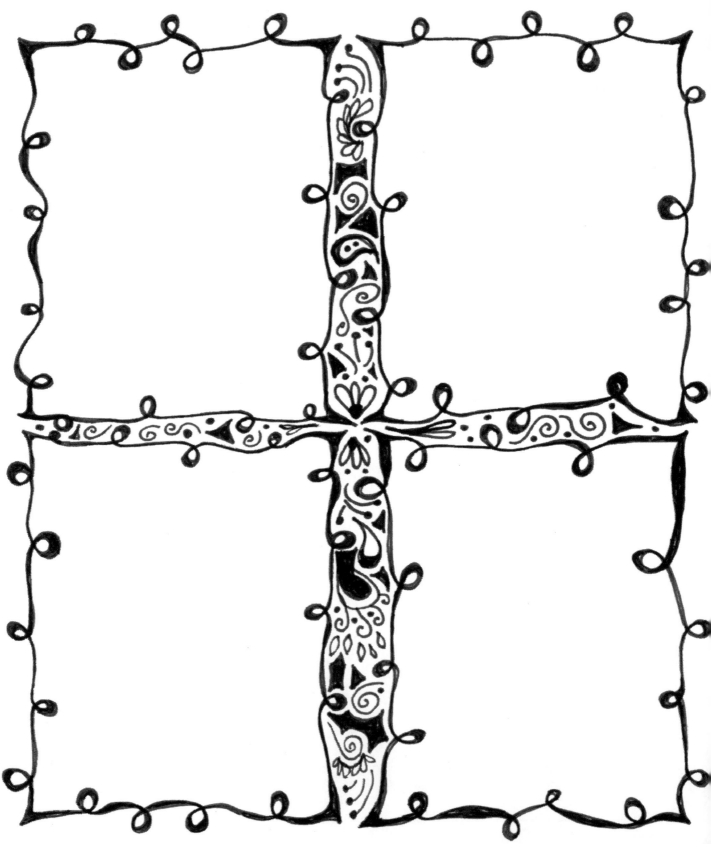

Copywork

Find an interesting paragraph in one of your books and copy it. Be diligent to make your writing look exactly like it does the book.

TITLE: _____

Page Number: _____

_____
_____
_____
_____
_____
_____
_____
_____
_____
_____
_____

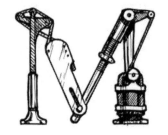

Math Practice

You can design something. You can make graphs, maps, or geometric designs. You can practice math problems.

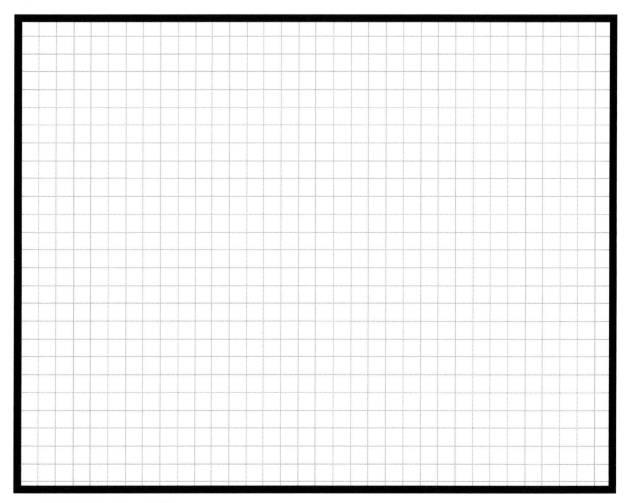

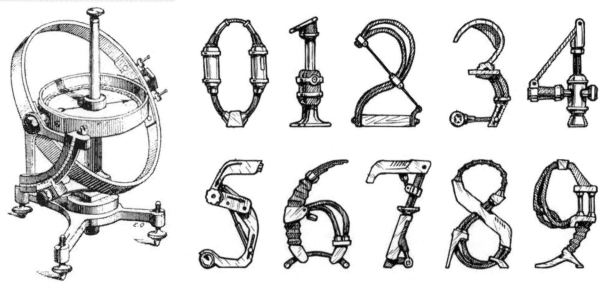

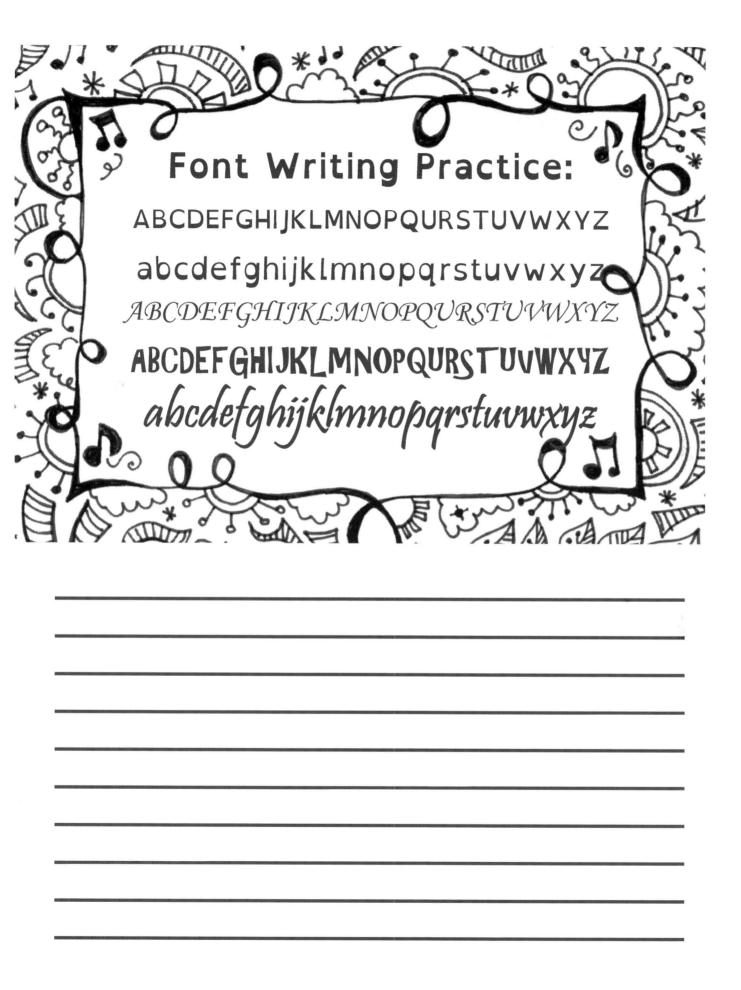

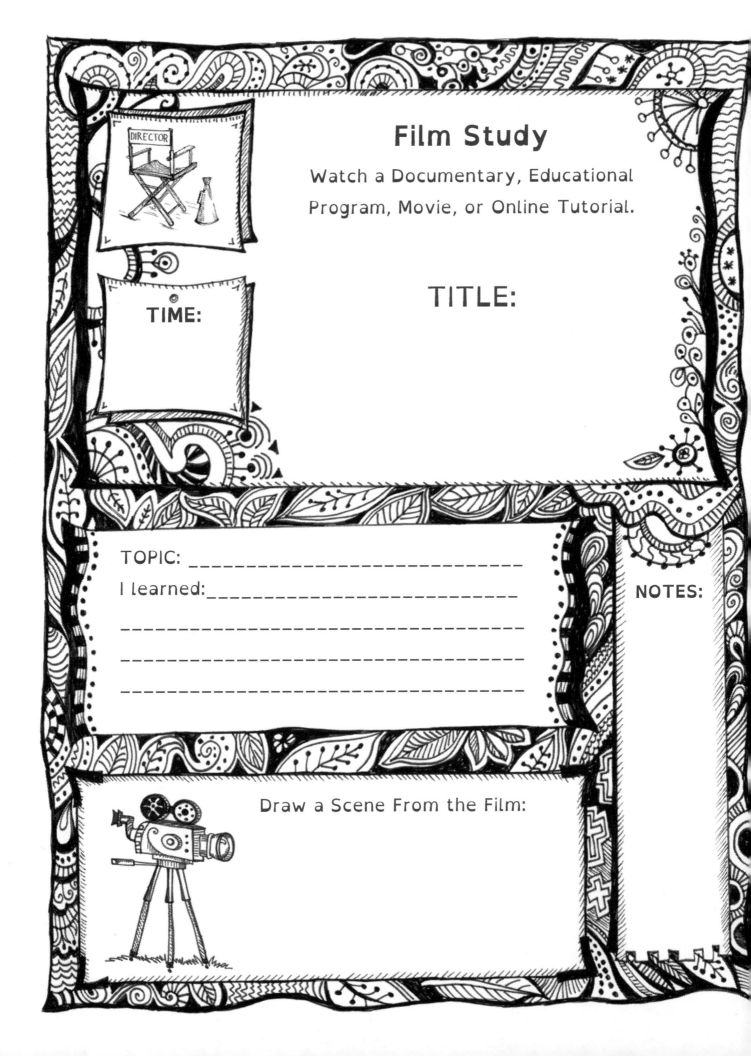

Spelling Time

Find 20 Words with 8 letters each.
Look in your books for words.
Write the words here:

Object Lesson

Look at this interesting object from the past.
Do you know what it is?

_____

What could it be used for?

_____
_____

How would the world be different
if this was not invented?

_____
_____
_____
_____
_____
_____
_____
_____
_____

Write down an inspirational quote:

To-Do List

Nature Study

Go outside and make a realistic drawing of something you find in in nature.

Reading Time - 1 Hour
Choose Four Books - Read from each book for 15 minutes.
Copy a sentence or picture from each book here:

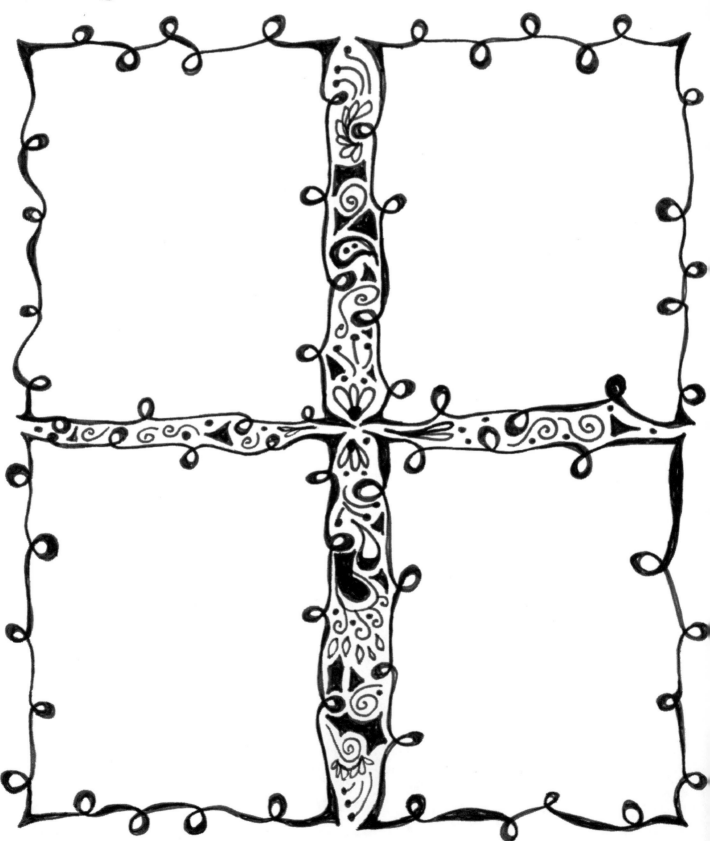

Copywork

Find an interesting paragraph in one of your books and copy it. Be diligent to make your writing look exactly like it does the book.

TITLE:_____

Page Number:_____

Emotions & Moods

How are your feeling today?
Color the facial expressions
to match today's moods.

Can you of three things that might help your mood improve?
1.
2.
3.

Listening Time

Listen to an audio book or classical music or ask someone to read a story to you while you color and draw on the next page.

What are you listening to?

_____

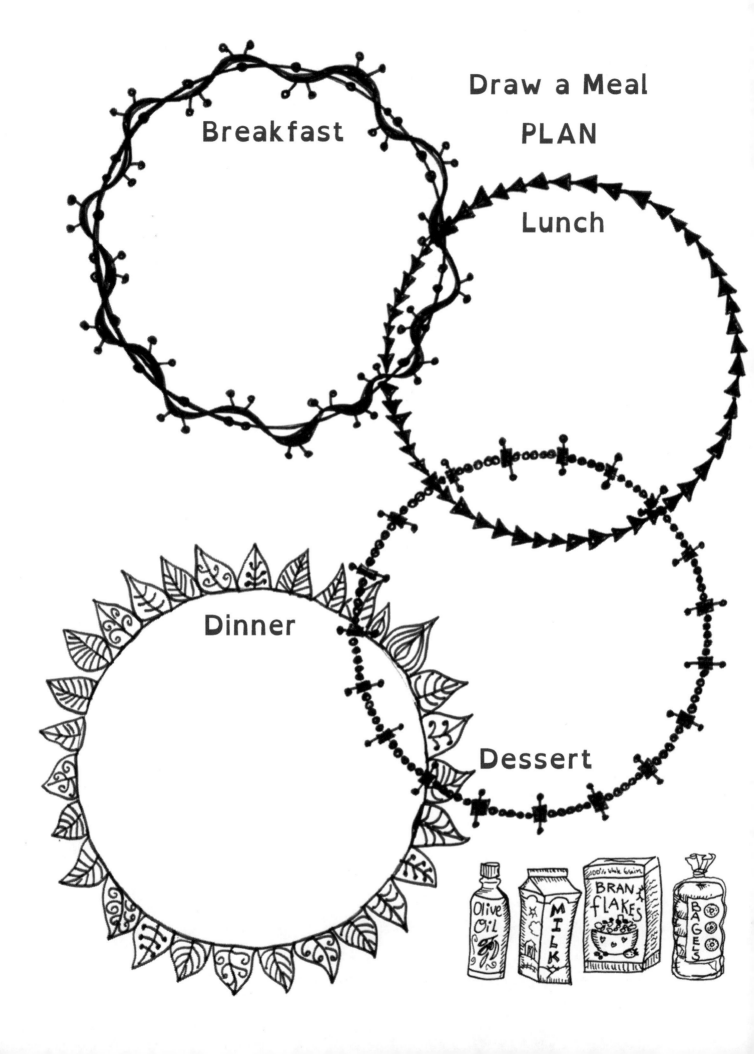

Recipe:

_____

Serves:

Prep Time:

Ingredients:

Instructions:

Shopping List:

Reading Time - 1 Hour

Choose Four Books - Read from each book for 15 minutes.
Copy a sentence or picture from each book here:

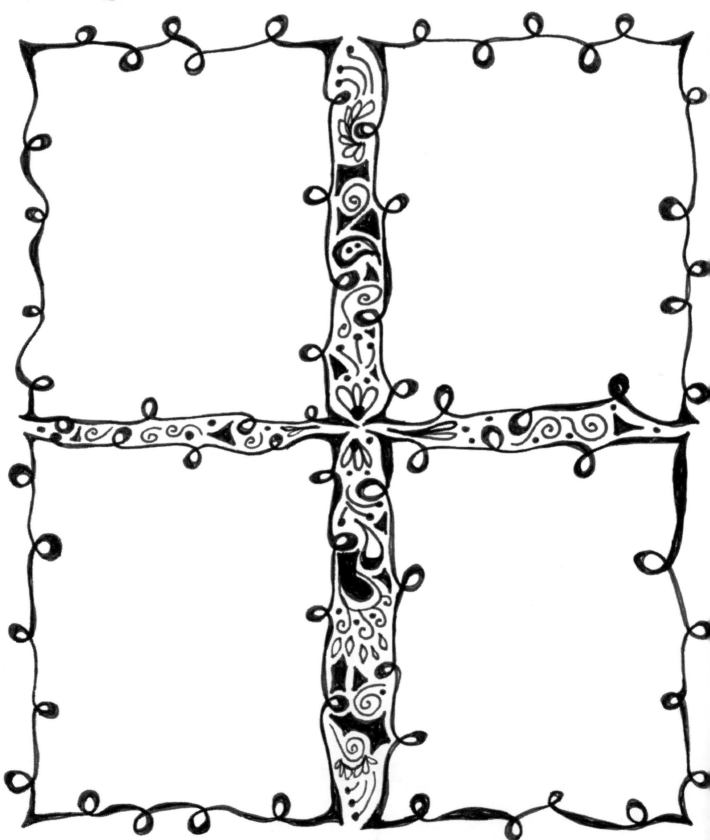

Copywork

Find an interesting paragraph in one of your books and copy it. Be diligent to make your writing look exactly like it does the book.

TITLE:_____

Page Number:_____

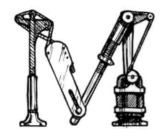

Math Practice

You can design something. You can make graphs, maps, or geometric designs. You can practice math problems.

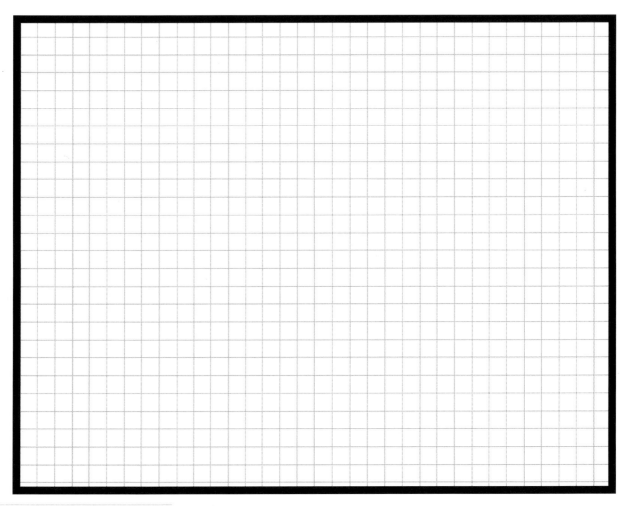

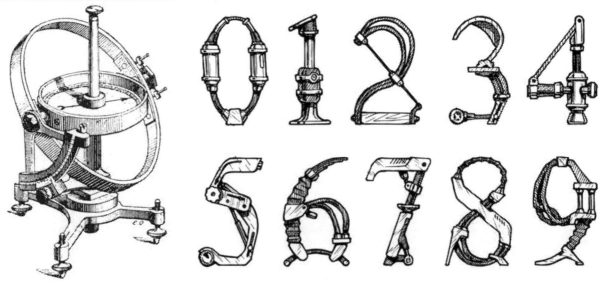

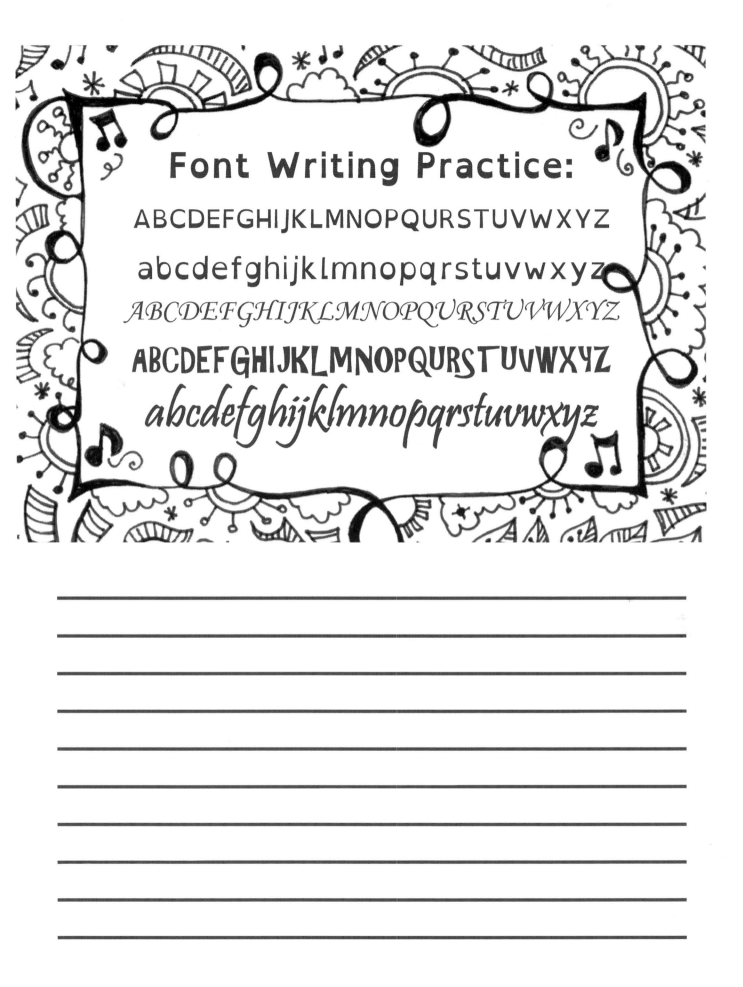

Font Writing Practice:

ABCDEFGHIJKLMNOPQURSTUVWXYZ

abcdefghijklmnopqrstuvwxyz

ABCDEFGHIJKLMNOPQURSTUVWXYZ

ABCDEFGHIJKLMNOPQURSTUVWXYZ

abcdefghijklmnopqrstuvwxyz

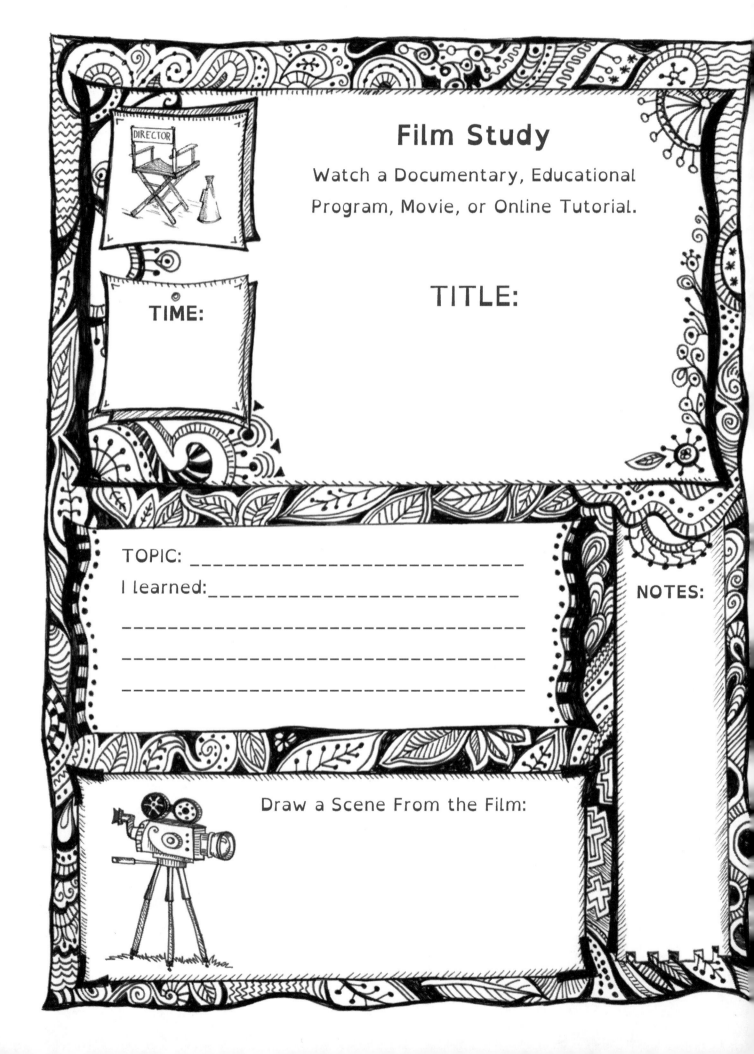

Spelling Time

Find 20 Words with 5 letters each.
Look in your books for words.
Write the words here:

Object Lesson

Look at this interesting object from the past.
Do you know what it is?

_____

What could it be used for?

_____
_____

How would the world be different
if this was not invented?

_____
_____
_____
_____
_____
_____
_____
_____
_____

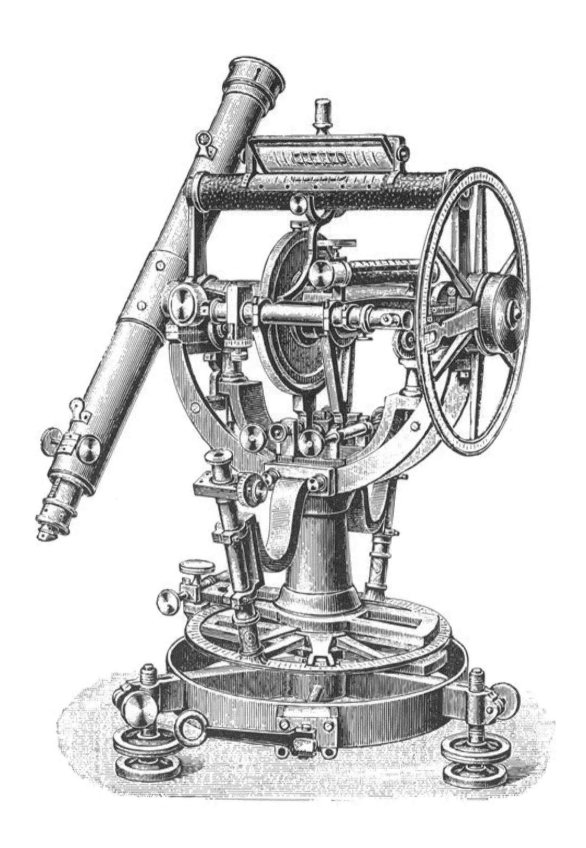

Nature Study

Go outside and make a realistic drawing of something you find in in nature.

Reading Time - 1 Hour

Choose Four Books - Read from each book for 15 minutes.
Copy a sentence or picture from each book here:

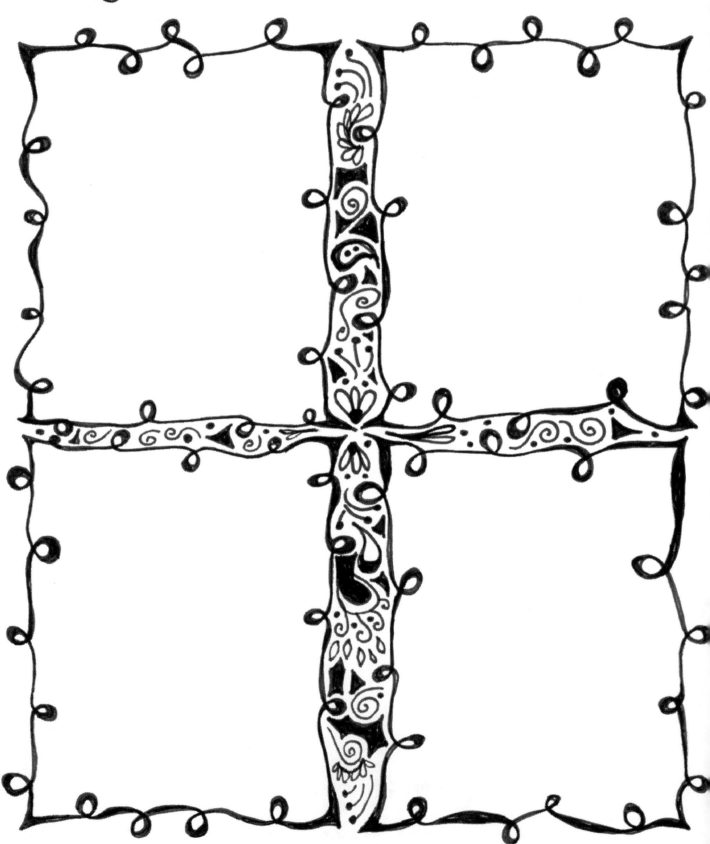

Copywork

Find an interesting paragraph in one of your books and copy it. Be diligent to make your writing look exactly like it does the book.

TITLE: _____

Page Number: _____

Emotions & Moods

How are your feeling today? Color the facial expressions to match today's moods.

Can you of three things that might help your mood improve?
1.
2.
3.

Listening Time

Listen to an audio book or classical music or ask someone to read a story to you while you color and draw on the next page.

What are you listening to?

_____

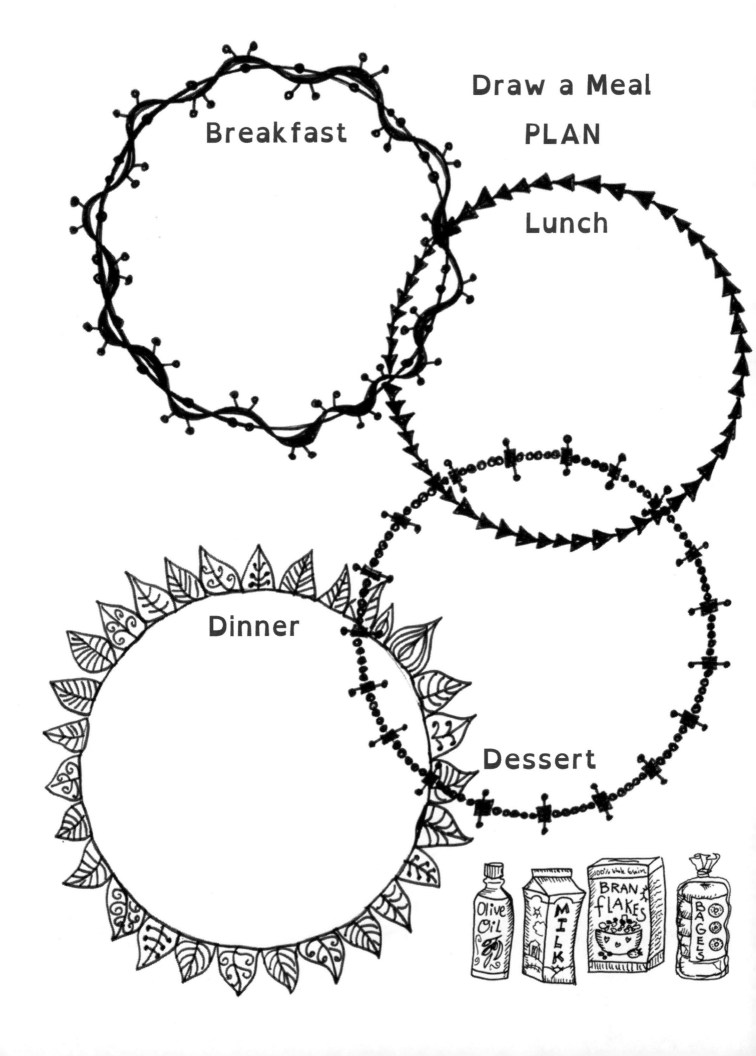

Recipe:

_____

Serves:

Prep Time:

Ingredients:

Instructions:

Shopping List:

Reading Time - 1 Hour

Choose Four Books - Read from each book for 15 minutes.
Copy a sentence or picture from each book here:

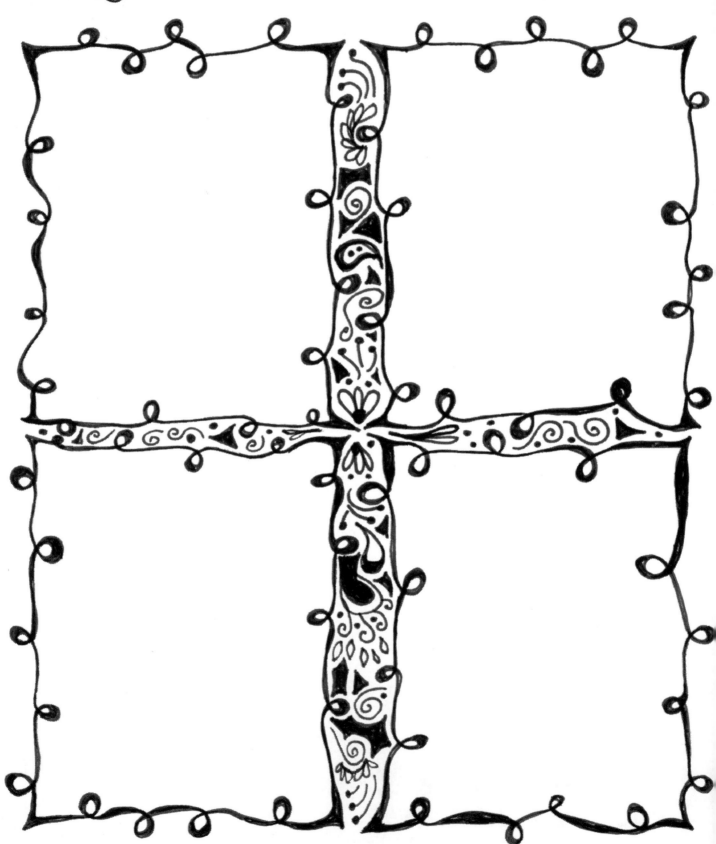

Copywork

Find an interesting paragraph in one of your books and copy it. Be diligent to make your writing look exactly like it does the book.

TITLE:_____

Page Number:_____

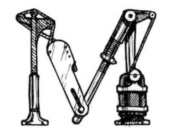

Math Practice

You can design something. You can make graphs, maps, or geometric designs. You can practice math problems.

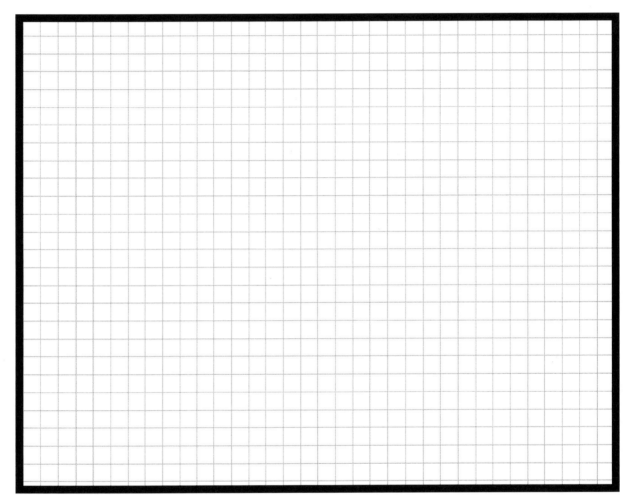

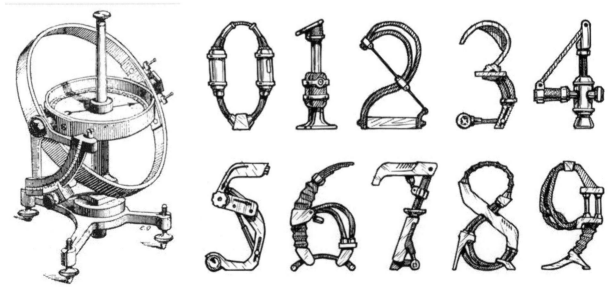

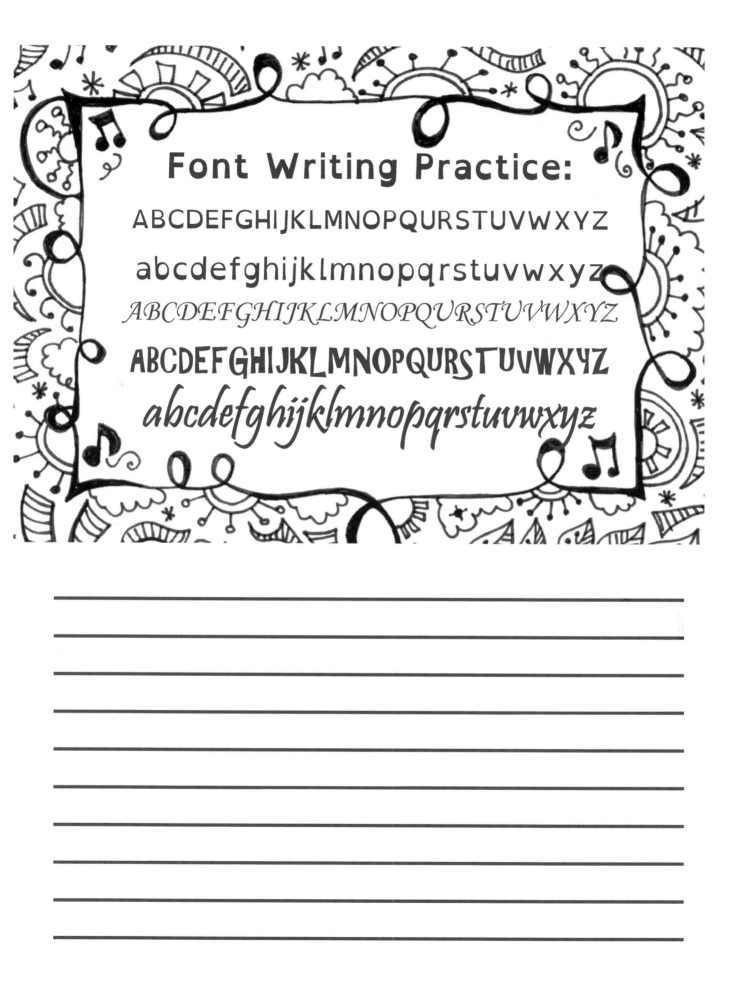

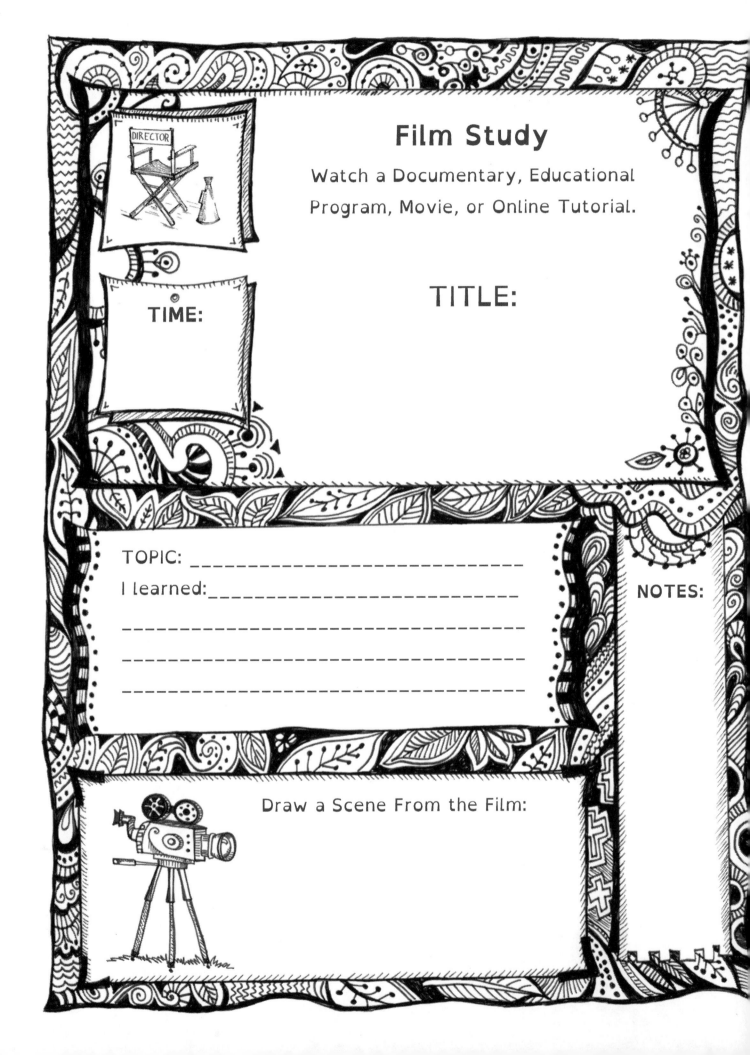

Spelling Time

Find 20 Words with ____ letters each.
Look in your books for words.
Write the words here:

Object Lesson

Look at this interesting object from the past.
Do you know what it is?

_____

What could it be used for?

_____
_____

How would the world be different
if this was not invented?

_____
_____
_____
_____
_____
_____
_____
_____
_____
_____

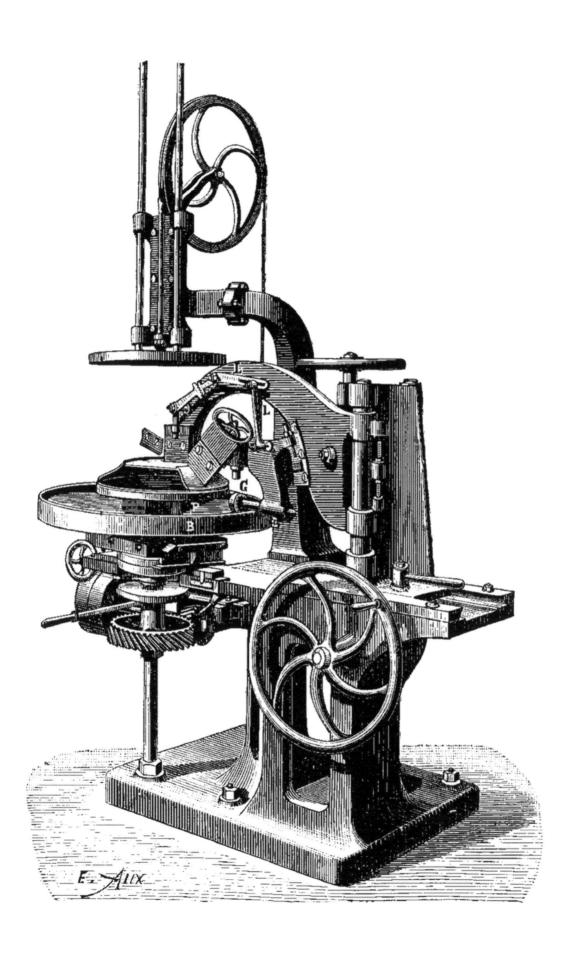

Write down an inspirational quote:

To-Do List

Nature Study
Go outside and make a realistic drawing of something you find in in nature.

Reading Time - 1 Hour
Choose Four Books - Read from each book for 15 minutes.
Copy a sentence or picture from each book here:

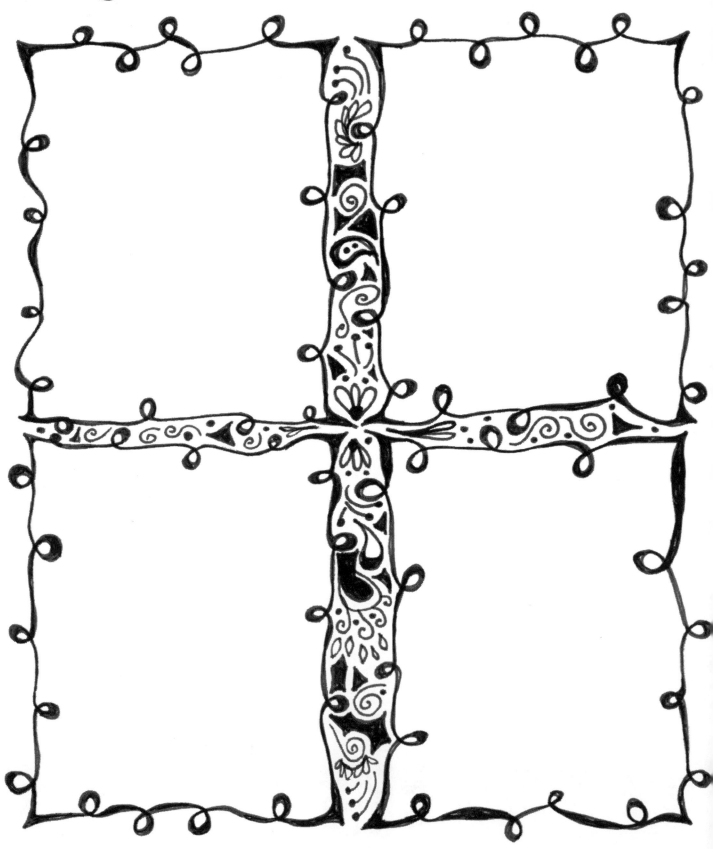

Copywork

Find an interesting paragraph in one of your books and copy it. Be diligent to make your writing look exactly like it does the book.

TITLE:_____

Page Number:_____

Emotions & Moods

How are your feeling today? Color the facial expressions to match today's moods.

Can you of three things that might help your mood improve?
1.
2.
3.

Listening Time

Listen to an audio book or classical music or ask someone to read a story to you while you color and draw on the next page.

What are you listening to?

_____

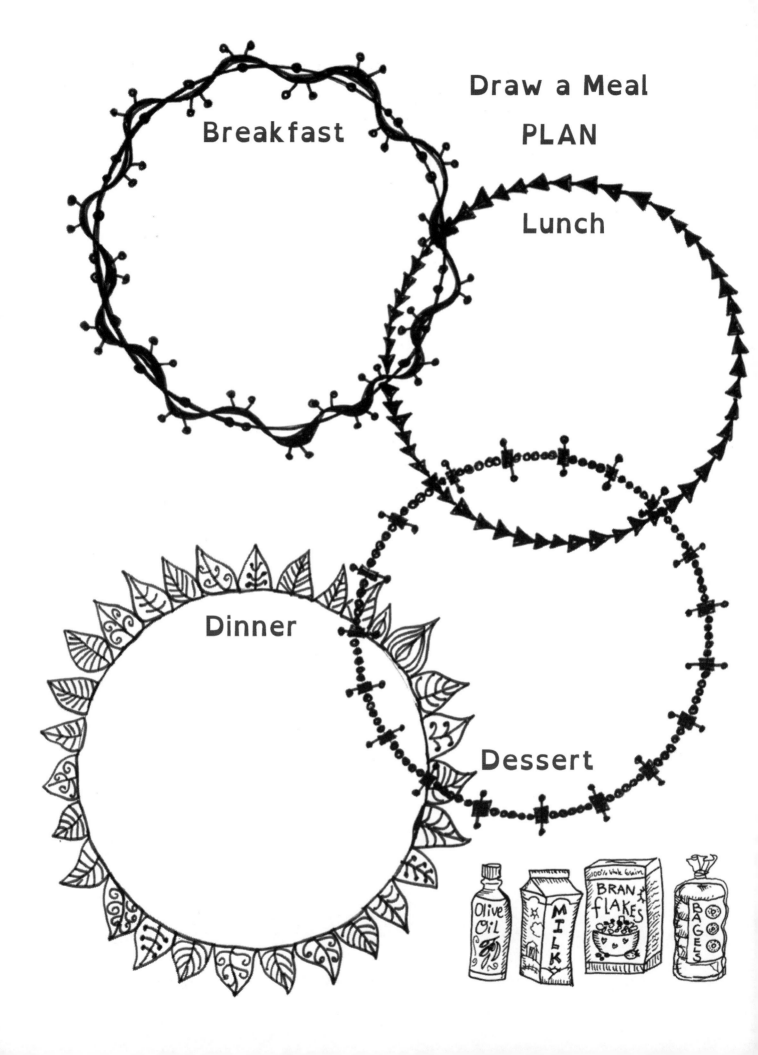

Recipe:

_____

Serves:

Prep Time:

Ingredients:

Instructions:

Shopping List:

Reading Time - 1 Hour
Choose Four Books - Read from each book for 15 minutes.
Copy a sentence or picture from each book here:

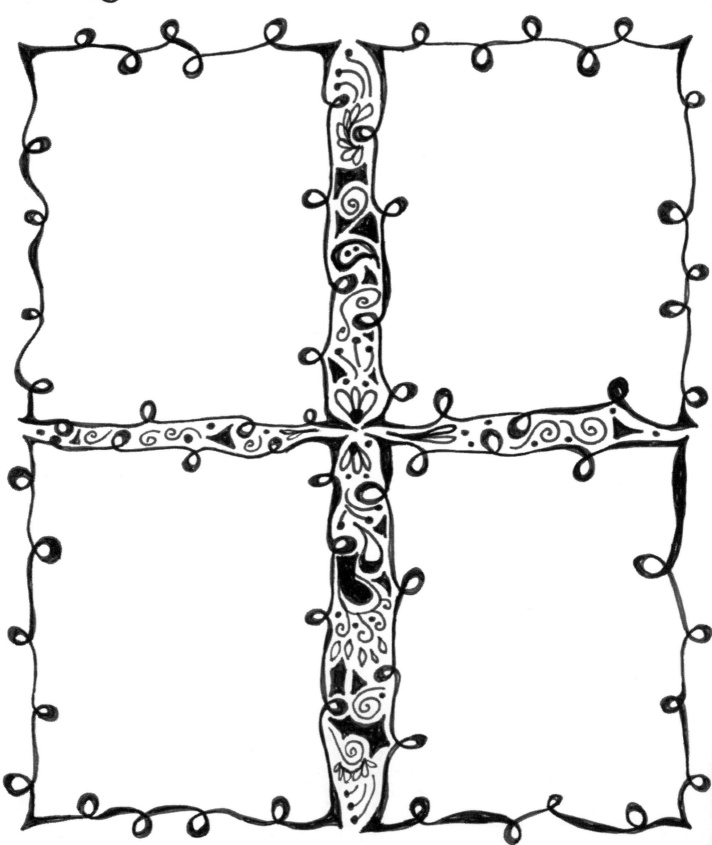

Copywork

Find an interesting paragraph in one of your books and copy it. Be diligent to make your writing look exactly like it does the book.

TITLE:_____

Page Number:_____

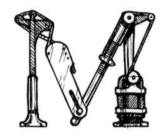

Math Practice

You can design something. You can make graphs, maps, or geometric designs. You can practice math problems.

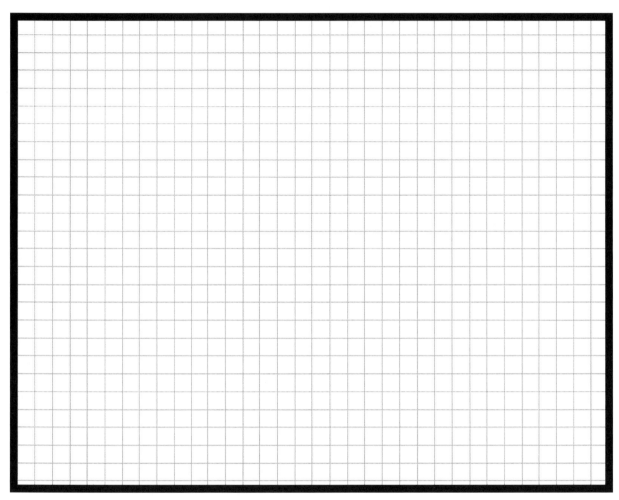

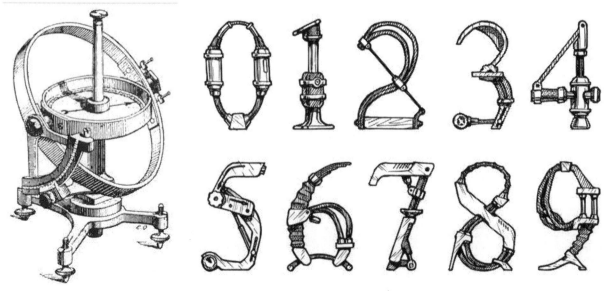

_____
_____
_____
_____
_____
_____
_____
_____
_____

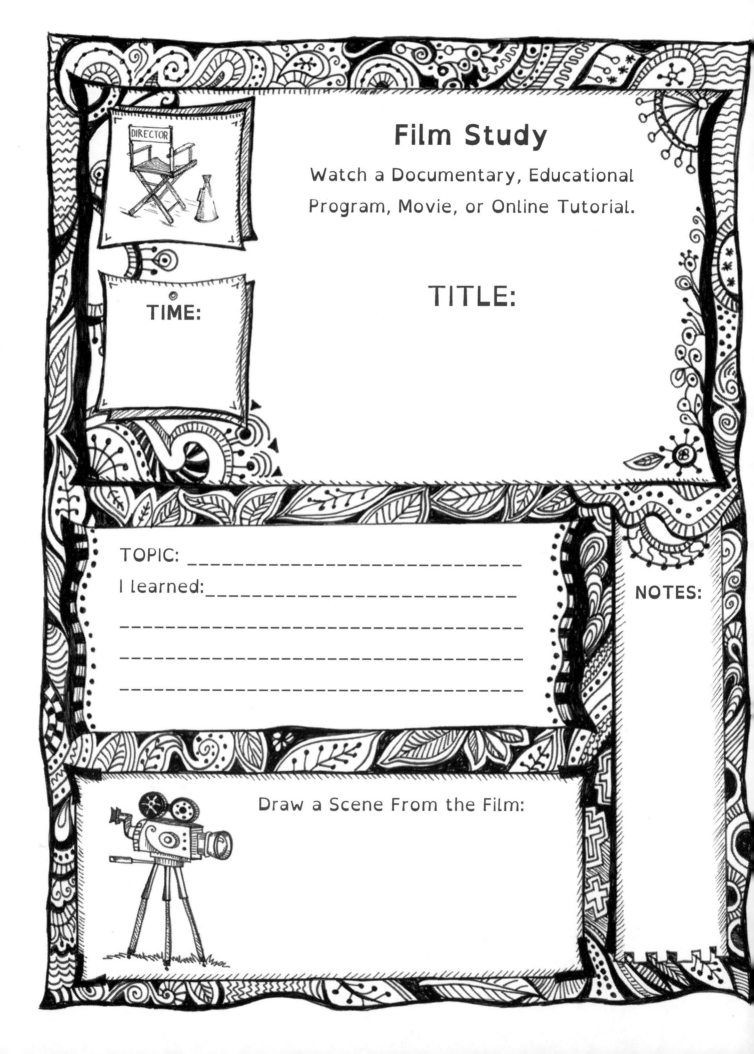

Object Lesson

Look at this interesting object from the past.
Do you know what it is?

_____

What could it be used for?

_____
_____

How would the world be different
if this was not invented?

_____
_____
_____
_____
_____
_____
_____
_____

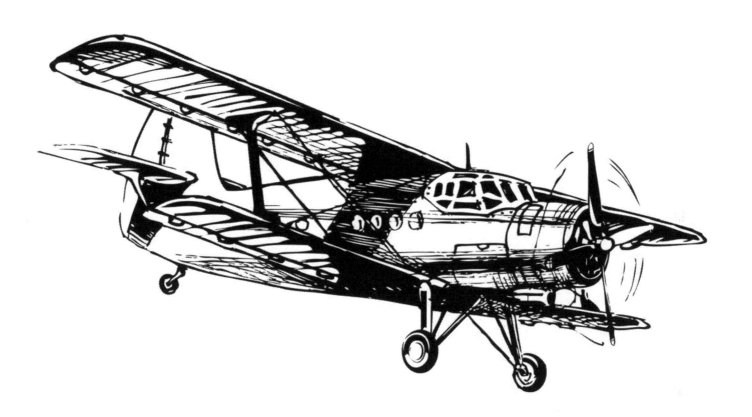

Write down an inspirational quote:

To-Do List

Nature Study

Go outside and make a realistic drawing of something you find in in nature.

Reading Time - 1 Hour

Choose Four Books - Read from each book for 15 minutes.
Copy a sentence or picture from each book here:

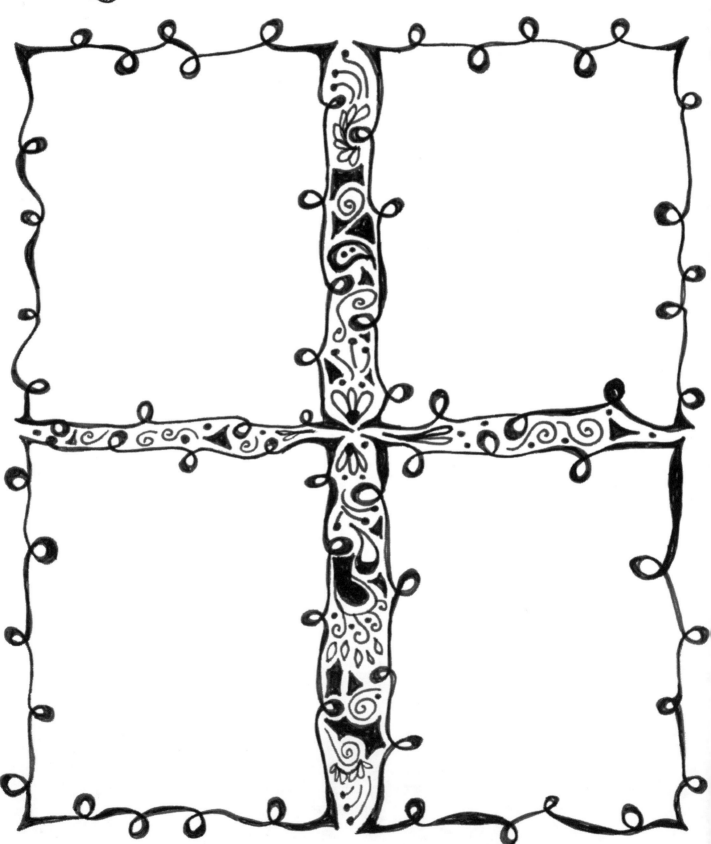

Copywork

Find an interesting paragraph in one of your books and copy it. Be diligent to make your writing look exactly like it does the book.

TITLE:_____

Page Number:_____

Emotions & Moods

How are your feeling today?
Color the facial expressions
to match today's moods.

Can you of three things that might help your mood improve?
1.
2.
3.

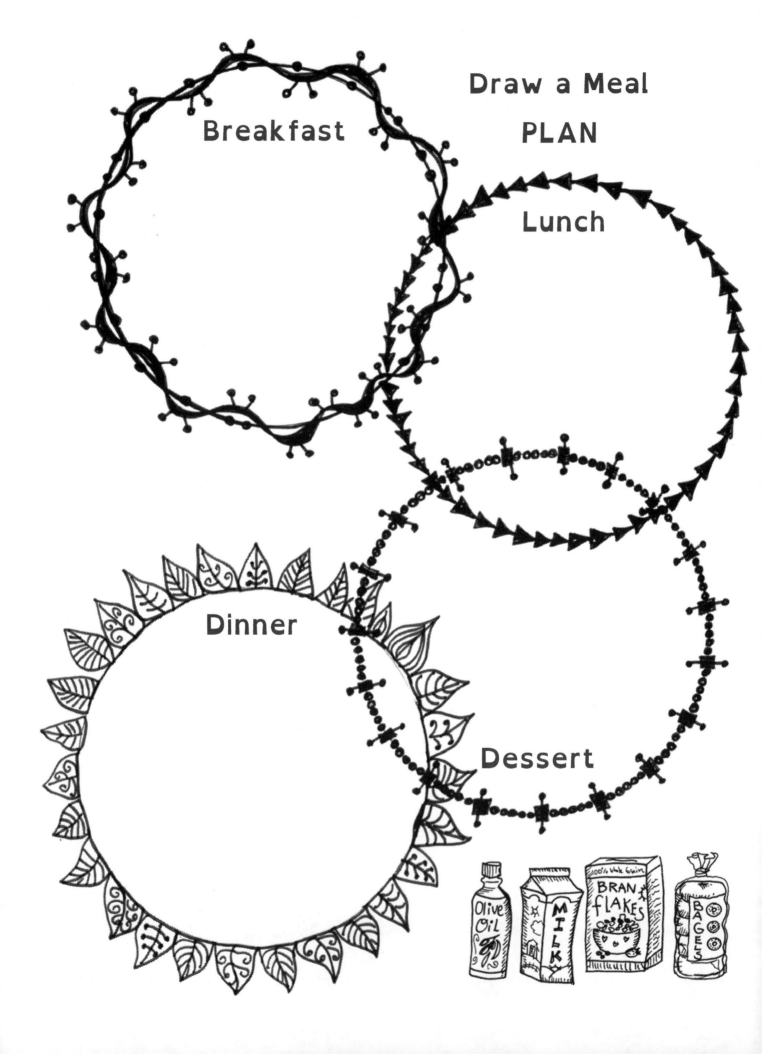

Recipe:

_____

Serves:

Prep Time:

Ingredients:

Instructions:

Shopping List:

Reading Time - 1 Hour

Choose Four Books - Read from each book for 15 minutes.
Copy a sentence or picture from each book here:

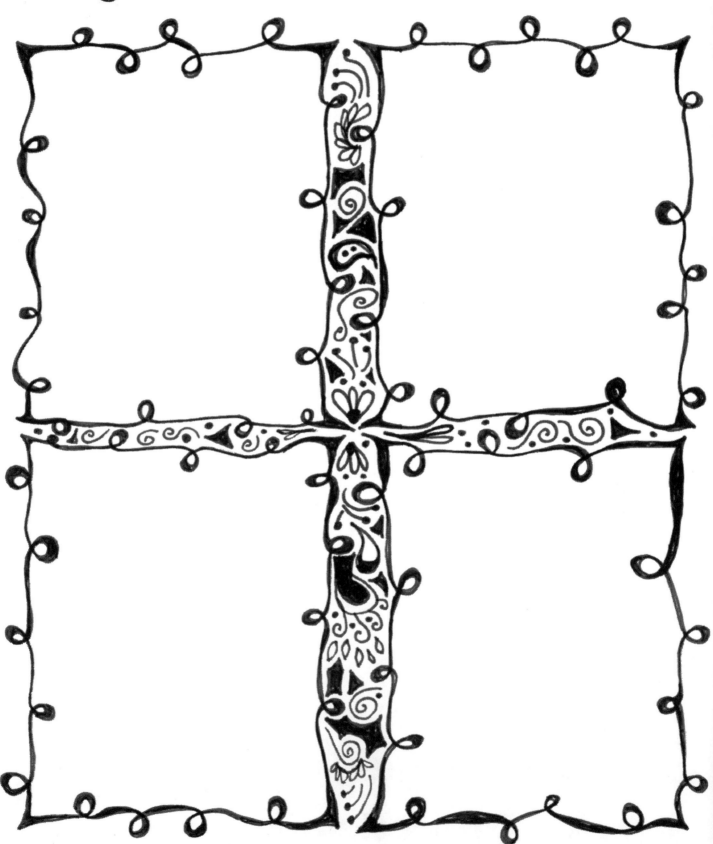

Copywork

Find an interesting paragraph in one of your books and copy it. Be diligent to make your writing look exactly like it does the book.

TITLE:_____

Page Number:_____

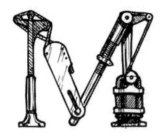

Math Practice

You can design something. You can make graphs, maps, or geometric designs. You can practice math problems.

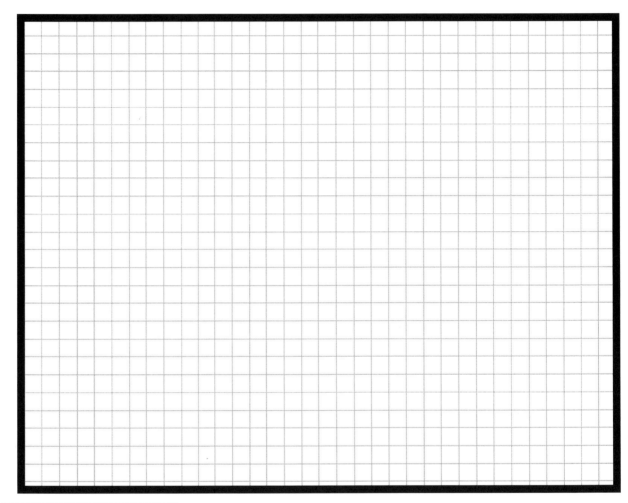

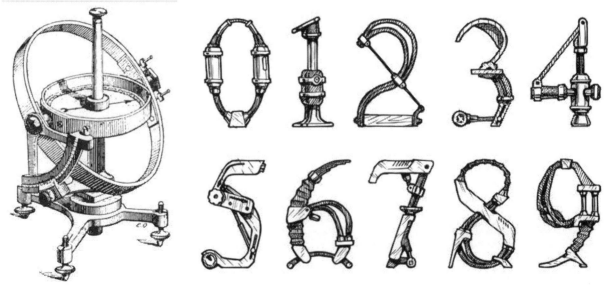

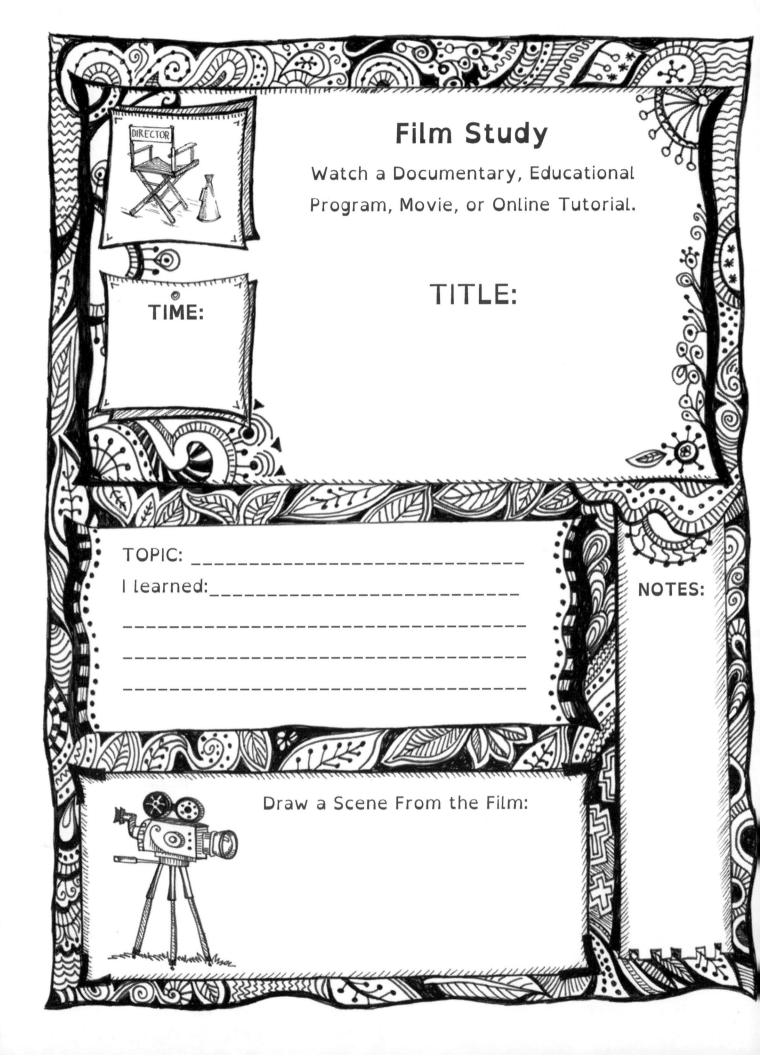

Object Lesson

Look at this interesting object from the past.
Do you know what it is?

_____

What could it be used for?

_____
_____

How would the world be different
if this was not invented?

_____
_____
_____
_____
_____
_____
_____
_____
_____

Write down an inspirational quote:

To-Do List

Nature Study
Go outside and make a realistic drawing of something you find in in nature.

Reading Time - 1 Hour

Choose Four Books - Read from each book for 15 minutes.
Copy a sentence or picture from each book here:

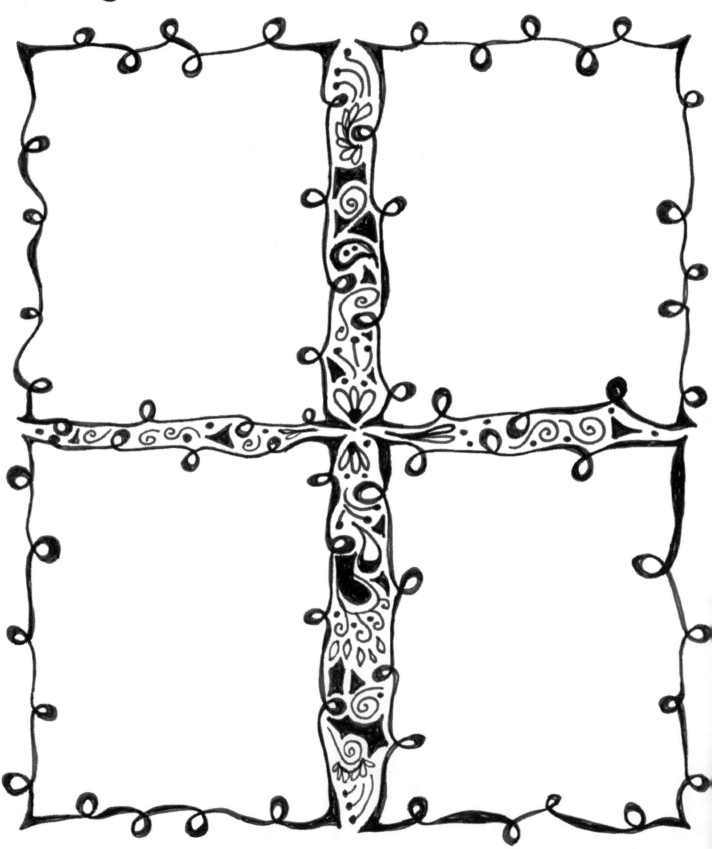

Copywork

Find an interesting paragraph in one of your books and copy it. Be diligent to make your writing look exactly like it does the book.

TITLE:_____

Page Number:_____

Emotions & Moods

How are your feeling today?
Color the facial expressions
to match today's moods.

Can you of three things that might help your mood improve?
1.
2.
3.

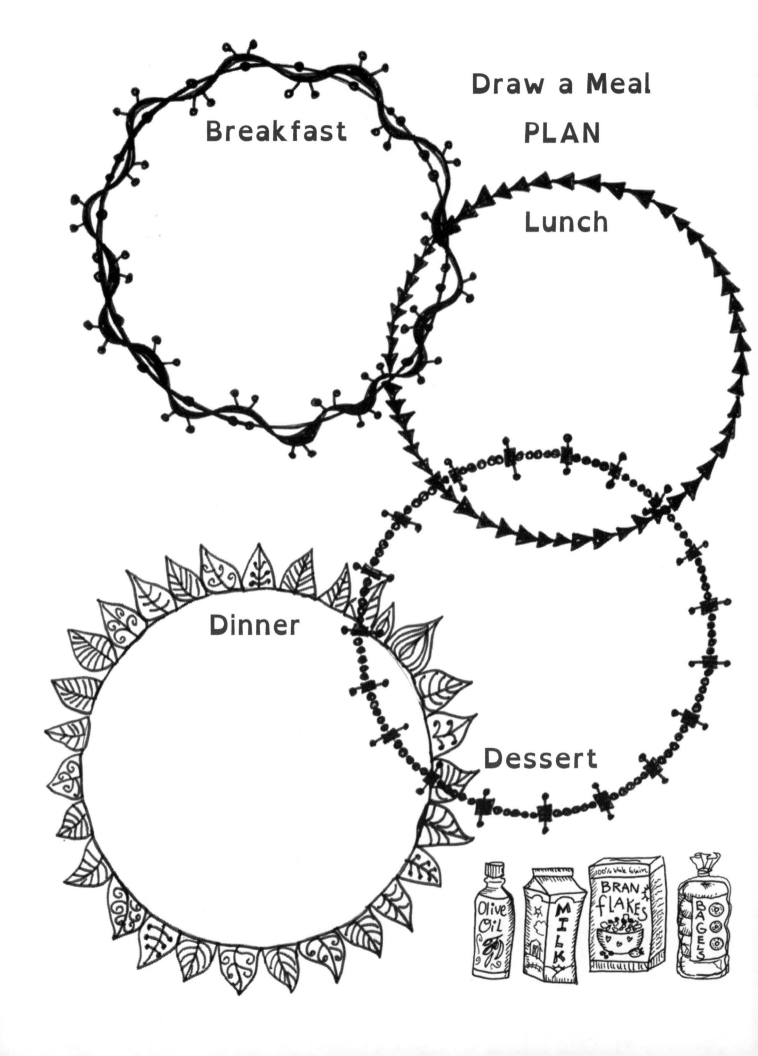

Recipe:

_____

Serves:

Prep Time:

Ingredients:

Instructions:

Shopping List:

Reading Time - 1 Hour

Choose Four Books - Read from each book for 15 minutes.
Copy a sentence or picture from each book here:

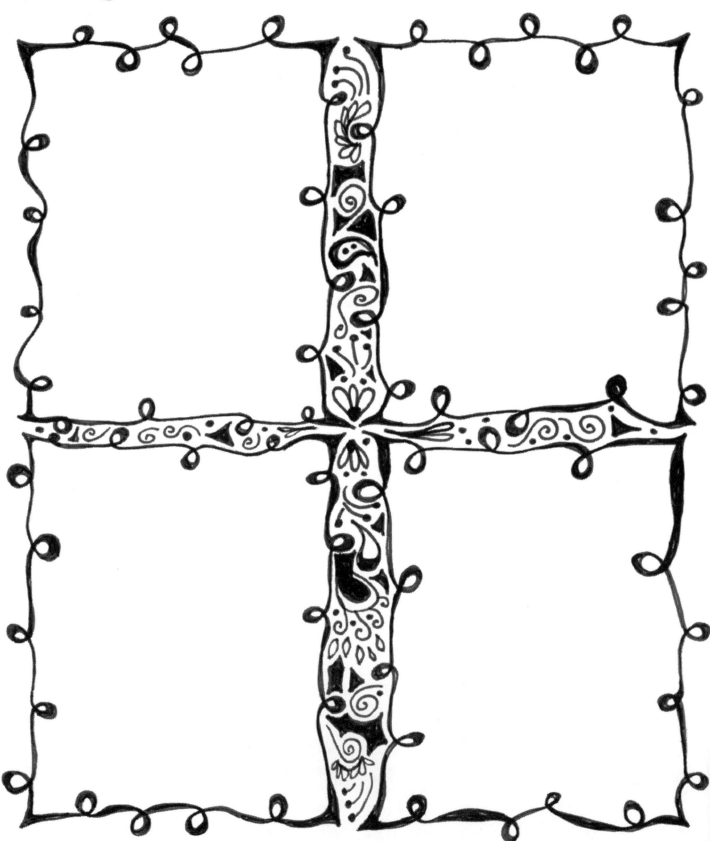

Copywork

Find an interesting paragraph in one of your books and copy it. Be diligent to make your writing look exactly like it does the book.

TITLE:_____

Page Number:_____

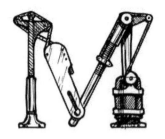

Math Practice

You can design something. You can make graphs, maps, or geometric designs. You can practice math problems.

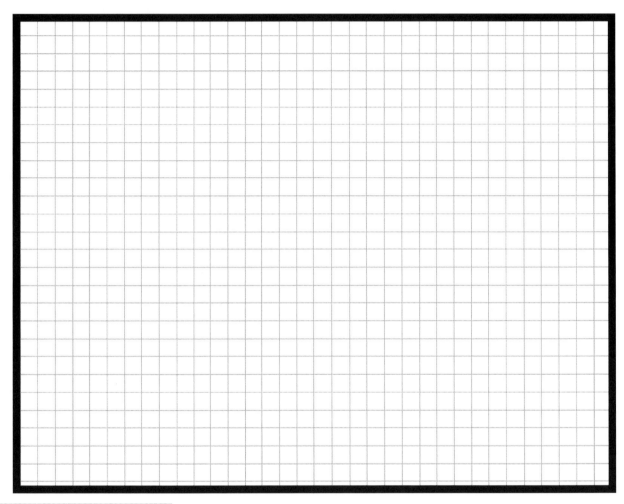

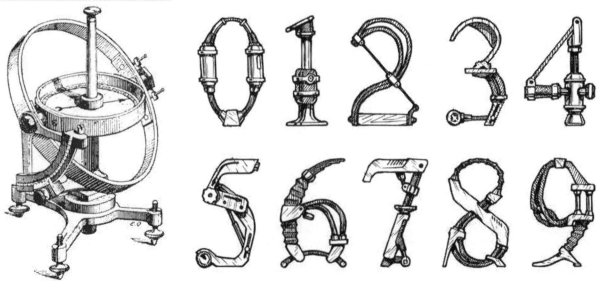

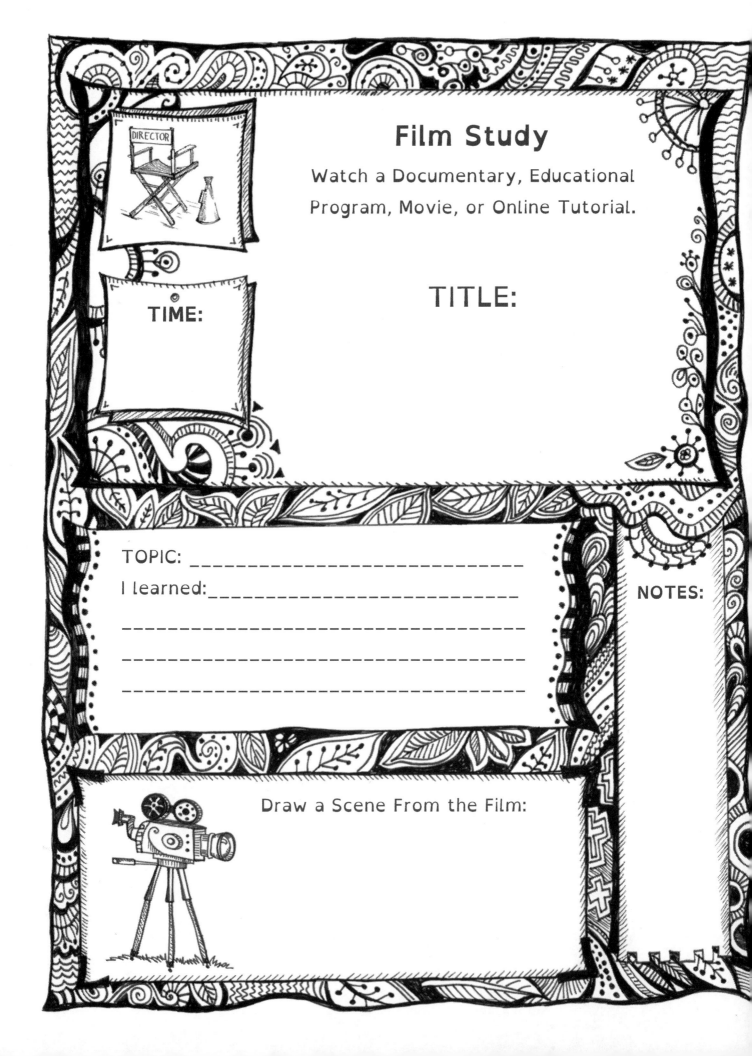

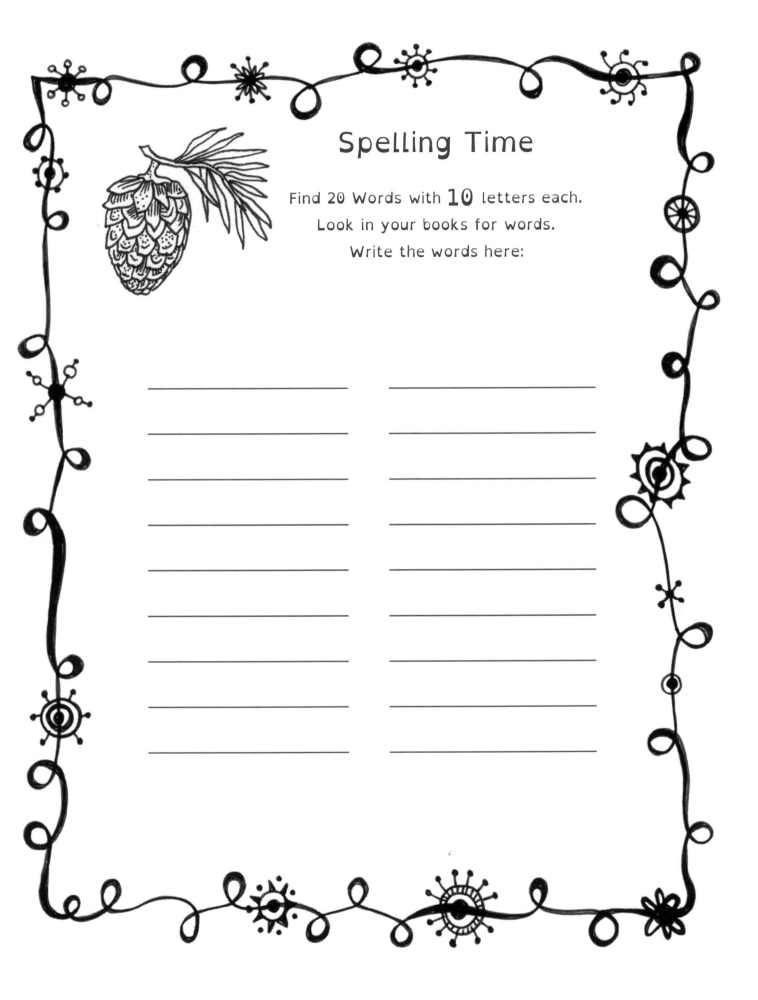

Spelling Time

Find 20 Words with **10** letters each.
Look in your books for words.
Write the words here:

Object Lesson

Look at this interesting object from the past.
Do you know what it is?

_____

What could it be used for?

_____
_____

How would the world be different
if this was not invented?

_____
_____
_____
_____
_____
_____
_____
_____
_____

Write down an inspirational quote:

To-Do List

Nature Study

Go outside and make a realistic drawing of something you find in in nature.

Reading Time - 1 Hour
Choose Four Books - Read from each book for 15 minutes.
Copy a sentence or picture from each book here:

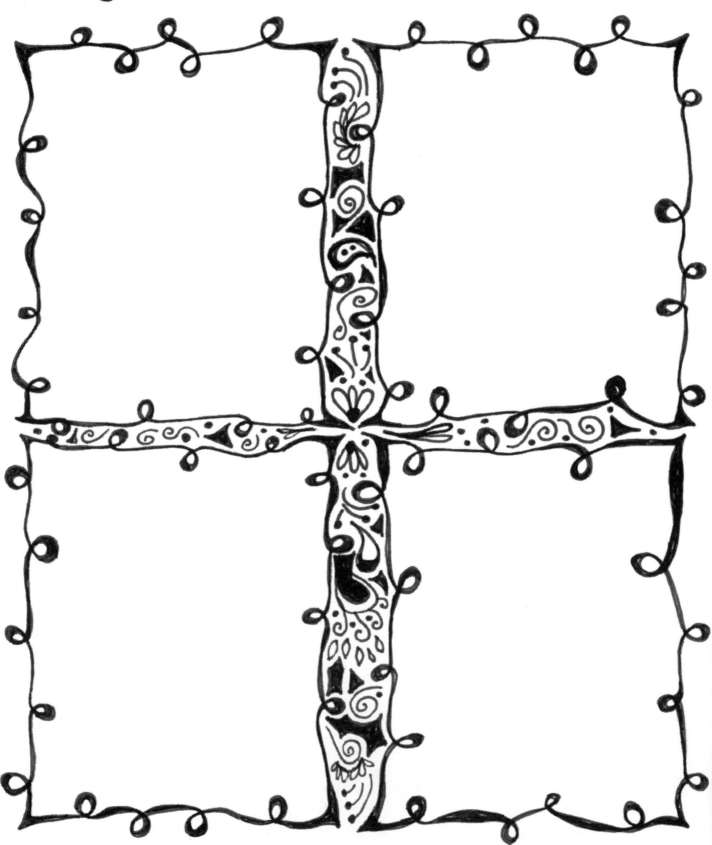

Copywork

Find an interesting paragraph in one of your books and copy it. Be diligent to make your writing look exactly like it does the book.

TITLE:_____

Page Number:_____

Emotions & Moods

How are your feeling today? Color the facial expressions to match today's moods.

Can you of three things that might help your mood improve?
1.
2.
3.

Listening Time

Listen to an audio book or classical music or ask someone to read a story to you while you color and draw on the next page.

What are you listening to?

_____

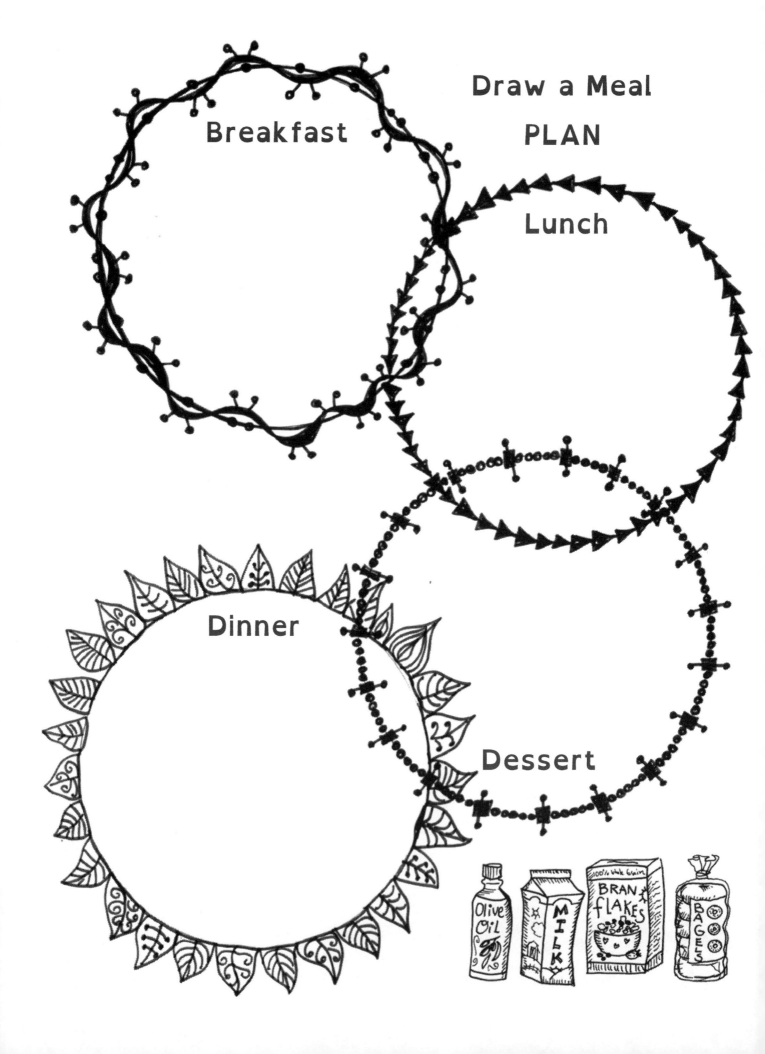

Recipe:

_____

Serves:

Prep Time:

Ingredients:

Instructions:

Shopping List:

Reading Time - 1 Hour

Choose Four Books - Read from each book for 15 minutes.
Copy a sentence or picture from each book here:

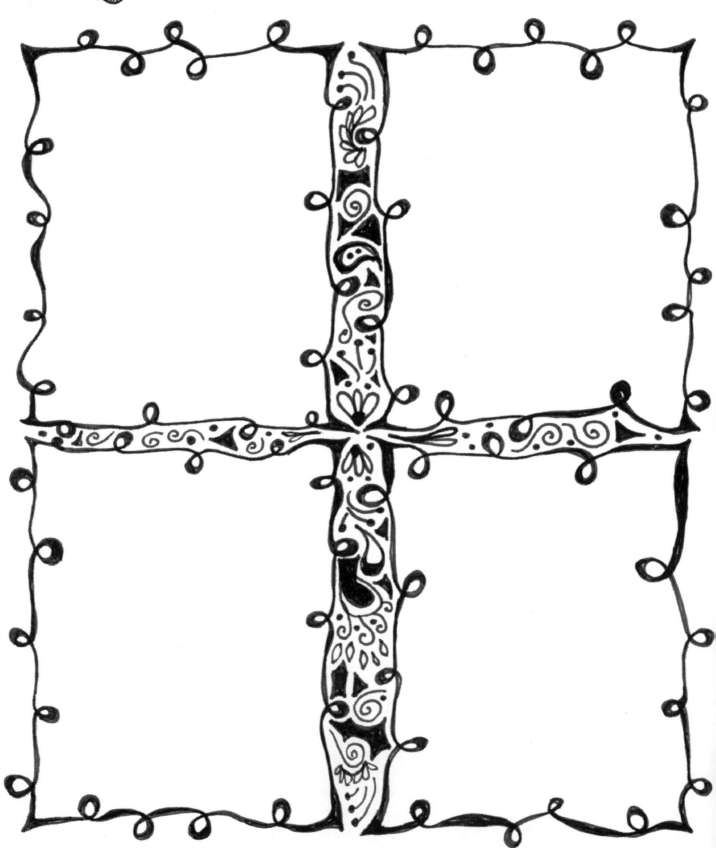

Copywork

Find an interesting paragraph in one of your books and copy it. Be diligent to make your writing look exactly like it does the book.

TITLE:_____

Page Number:_____

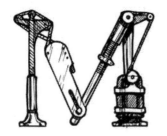

Math Practice

You can design something. You can make graphs, maps, or geometric designs. You can practice math problems.

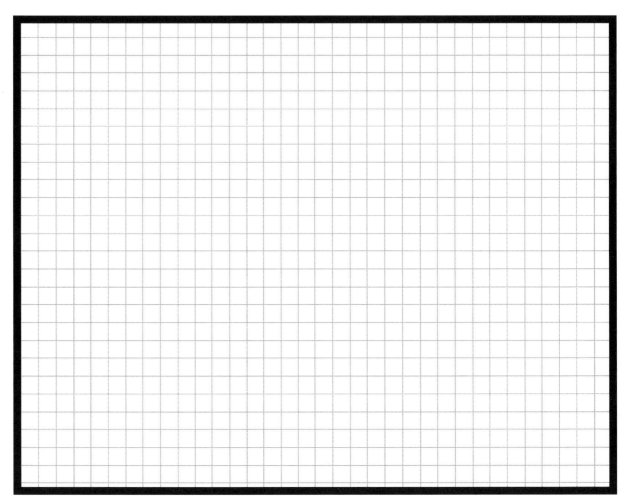

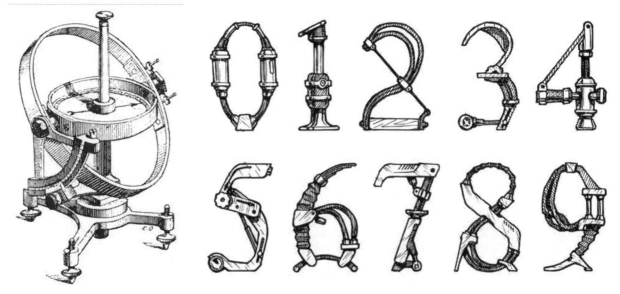

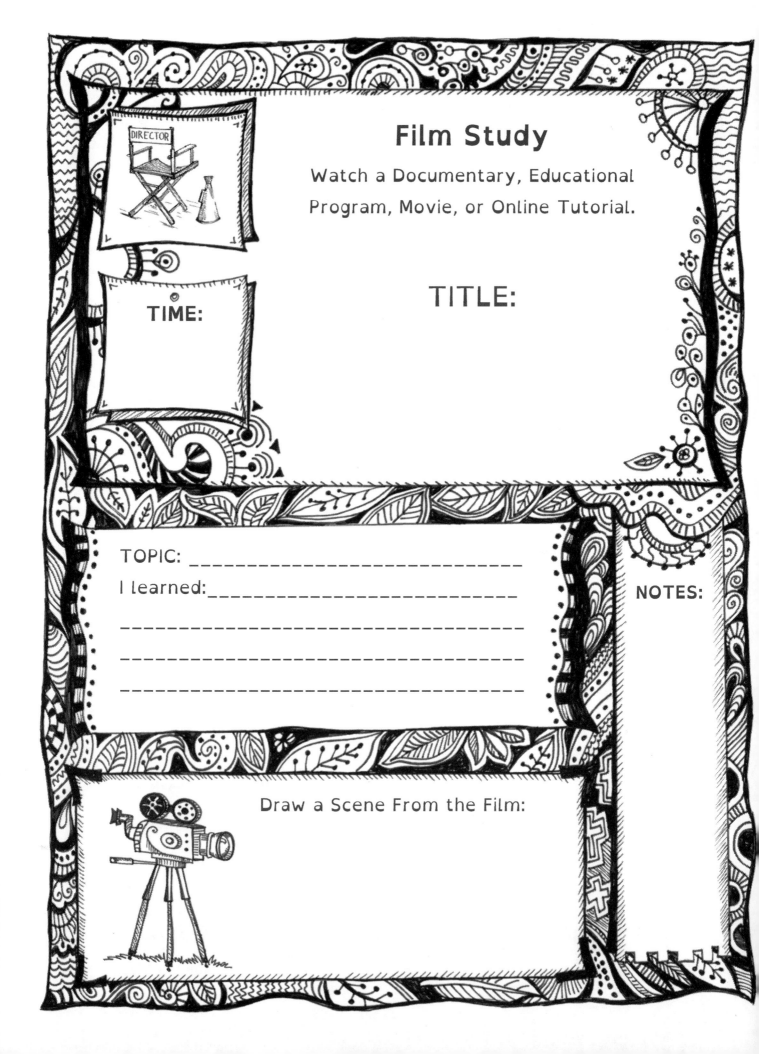

Spelling Time

Find 20 Words with 8 letters each.
Look in your books for words.
Write the words here:

Object Lesson

Look at this interesting object from the past.
Do you know what it is?

_____

What could it be used for?

_____
_____

How would the world be different
if this was not invented?

_____
_____
_____
_____
_____
_____
_____
_____
_____

Write down an inspirational quote:

To-Do List

Nature Study

Go outside and make a realistic drawing of something you find in in nature.

Reading Time - 1 Hour

Choose Four Books - Read from each book for 15 minutes.
Copy a sentence or picture from each book here:

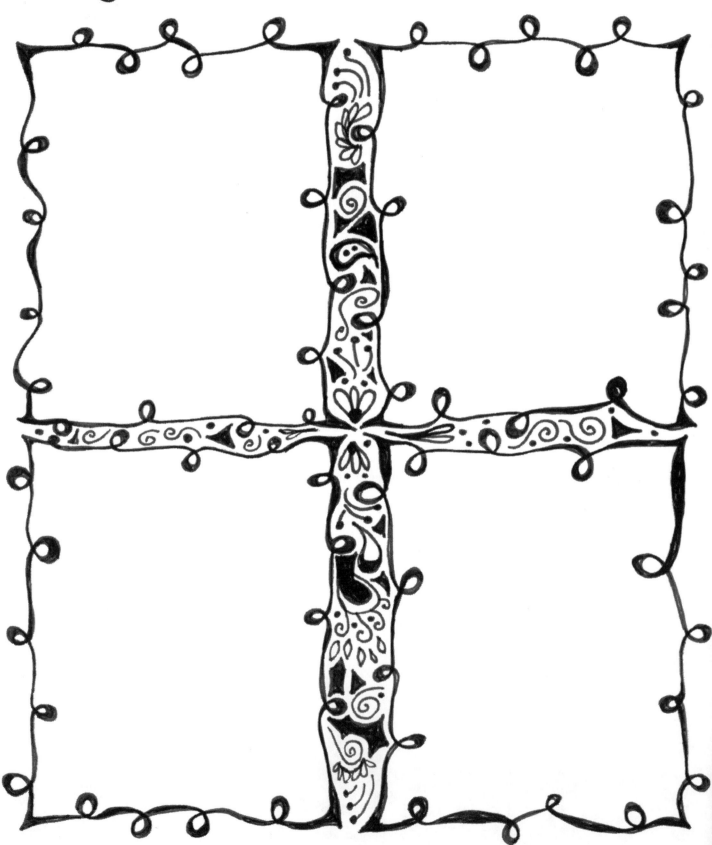

Copywork

Find an interesting paragraph in one of your books and copy it. Be diligent to make your writing look exactly like it does the book.

TITLE:_____

Page Number:_____

_____
_____
_____
_____
_____
_____
_____
_____
_____
_____
_____

Emotions & Moods

How are your feeling today?
Color the facial expressions
to match today's moods.

Can you of three things that might help your mood improve?
1.
2.
3.

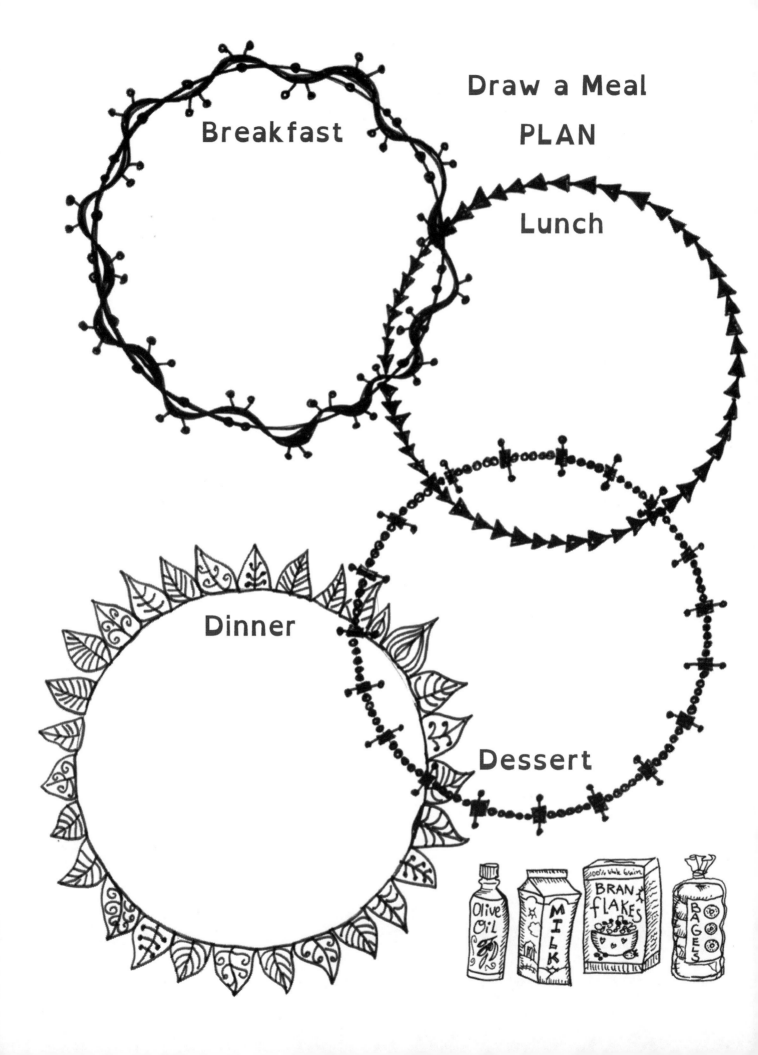

Recipe:

_____

Serves:

Prep Time:

Ingredients:

Instructions:

Shopping List:

Reading Time - 1 Hour
Choose Four Books - Read from each book for 15 minutes.
Copy a sentence or picture from each book here:

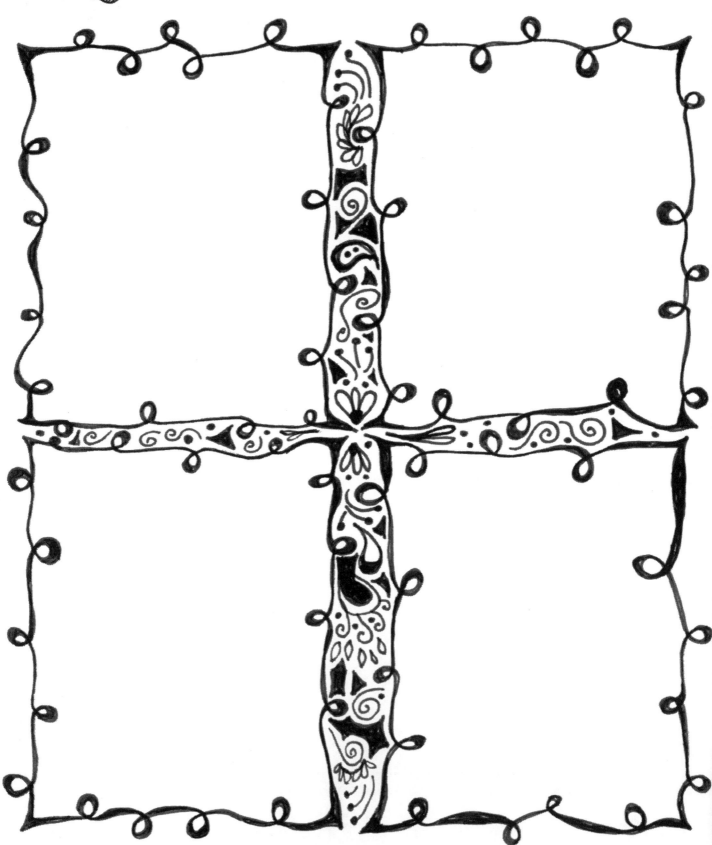

Copywork

Find an interesting paragraph in one of your books and copy it. Be diligent to make your writing look exactly like it does the book.

TITLE:_____

Page Number:_____

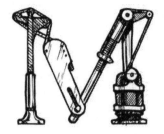

Math Practice

You can design something. You can make graphs, maps, or geometric designs. You can practice math problems.

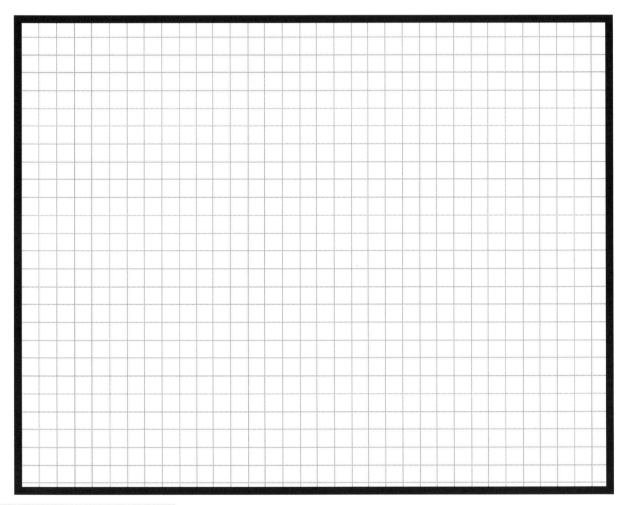

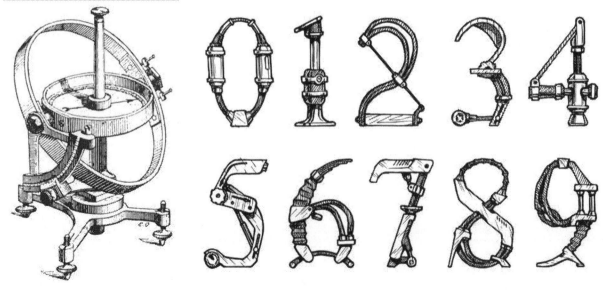

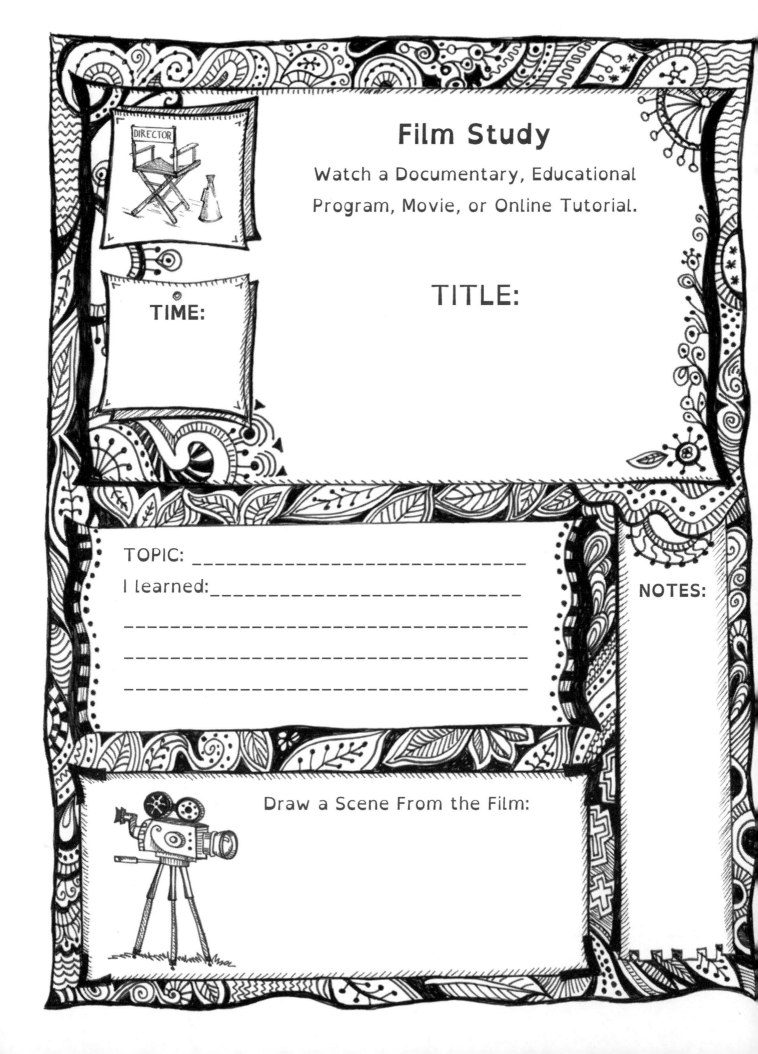

Spelling Time

Find 20 Words with 6 letters each.
Look in your books for words.
Write the words here:

Object Lesson

Look at this interesting object from the past.
Do you know what it is?

_____

What could it be used for?

_____
_____

How would the world be different
if this was not invented?

_____
_____
_____
_____
_____
_____
_____
_____
_____

Nature Study

Go outside and make a realistic drawing of something you find in in nature.

Reading Time - 1 Hour

Choose Four Books - Read from each book for 15 minutes.
Copy a sentence or picture from each book here:

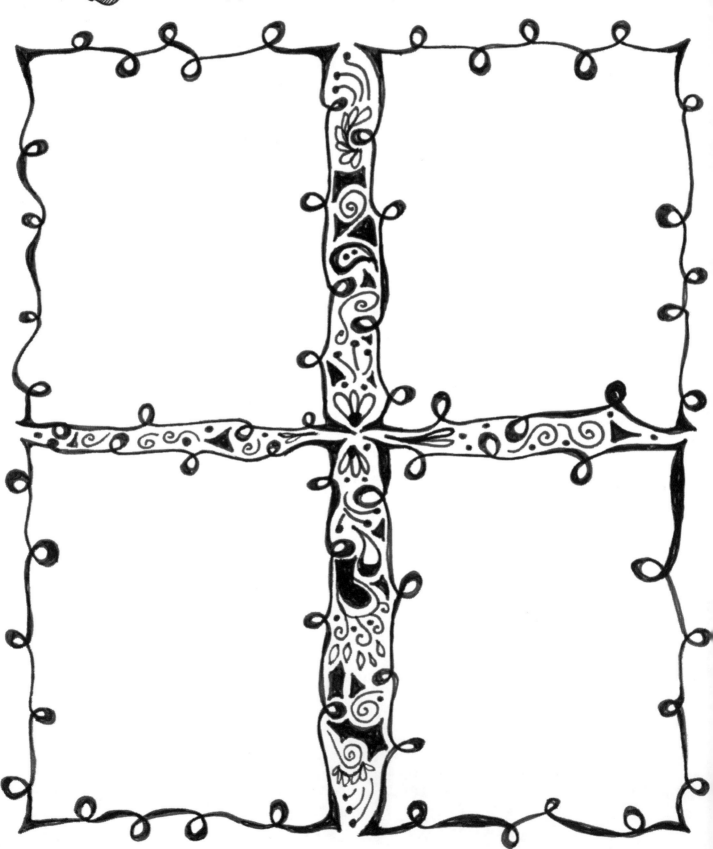

Copywork

Find an interesting paragraph in one of your books and copy it. Be diligent to make your writing look exactly like it does the book.

TITLE: _____

Page Number: _____

Emotions & Moods

How are your feeling today? Color the facial expressions to match today's moods.

Can you of three things that might help your mood improve?
1.
2.
3.

Listening Time

Listen to an audio book or classical music or ask someone to read a story to you while you color and draw on the next page.

What are you listening to?

_____

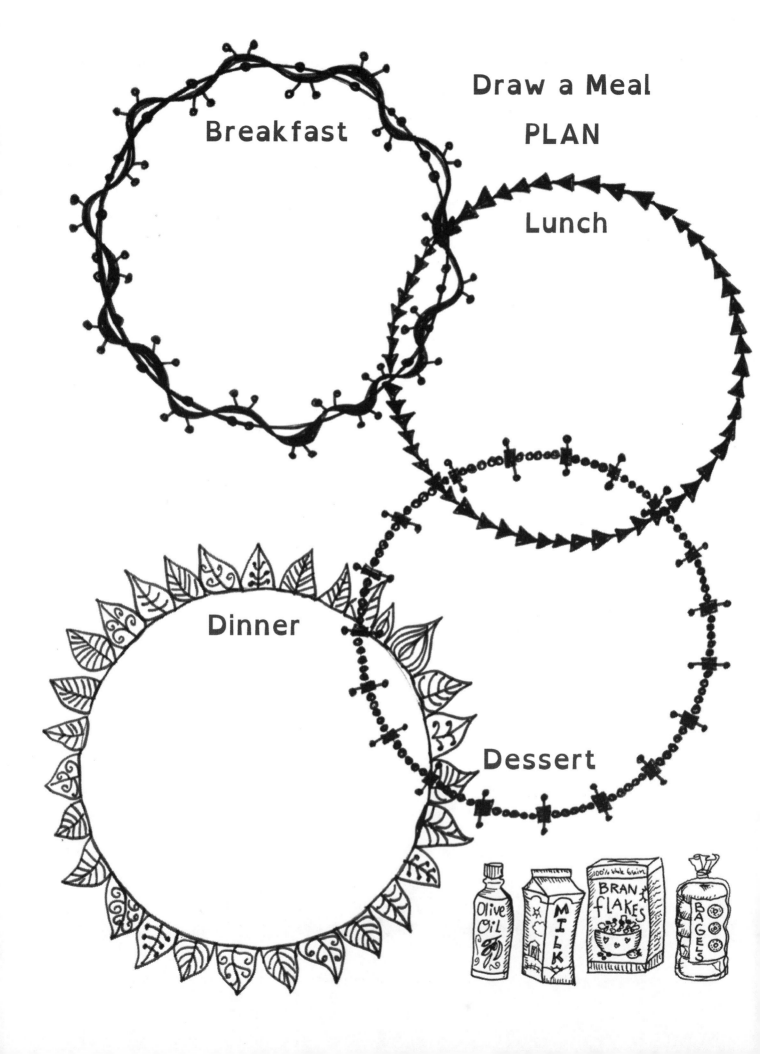

Recipe:

_____

Serves:

Prep Time:

Ingredients:

Instructions:

Shopping List:

Reading Time - 1 Hour
Choose Four Books - Read from each book for 15 minutes.
Copy a sentence or picture from each book here:

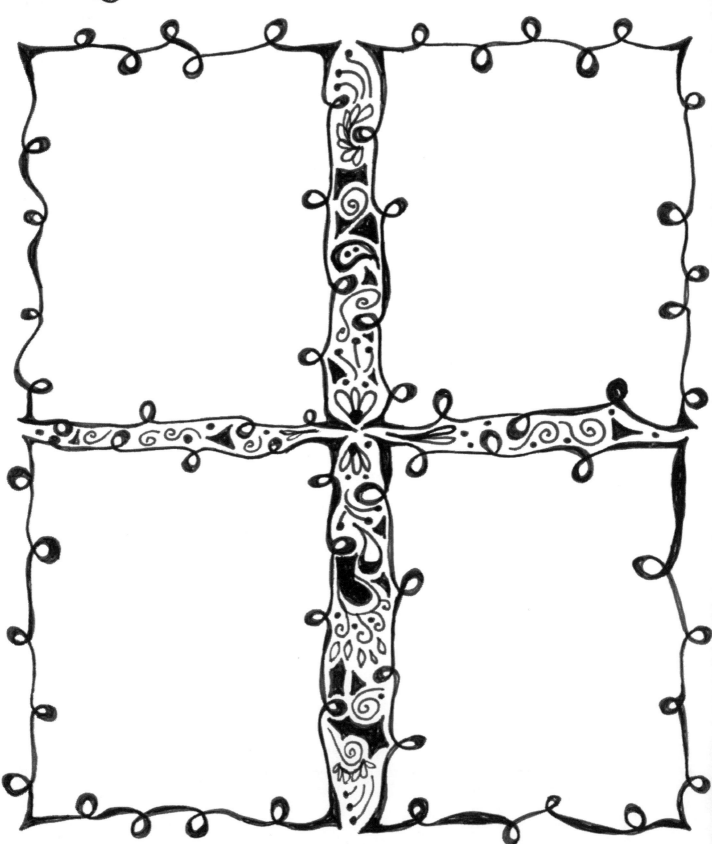

Copywork

Find an interesting paragraph in one of your books and copy it. Be diligent to make your writing look exactly like it does the book.

TITLE: _____

Page Number: _____

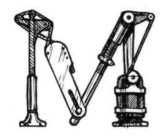

Math Practice

You can design something. You can make graphs, maps, or geometric designs. You can practice math problems.

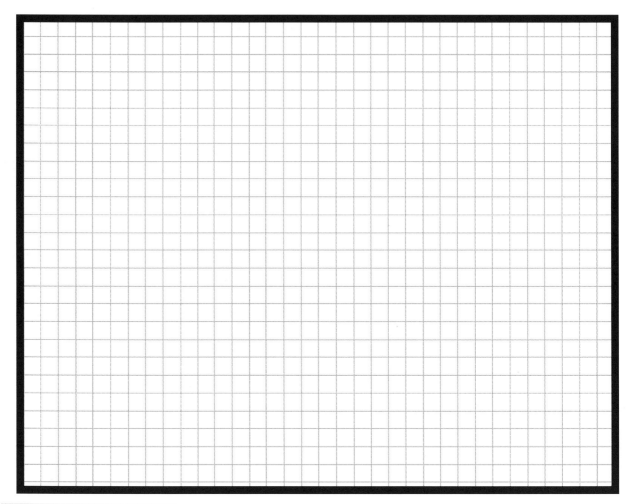

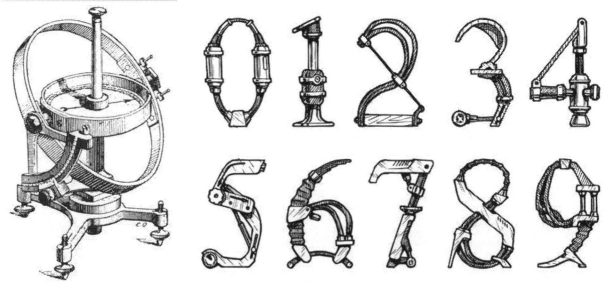

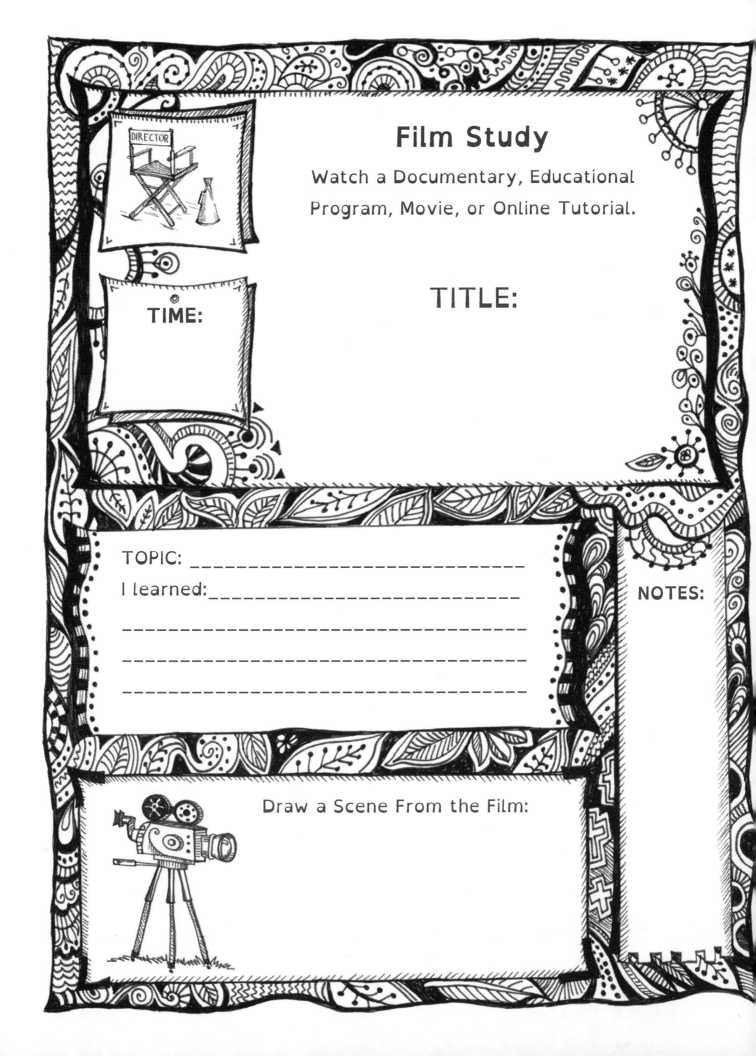

Object Lesson

Look at this interesting object from the past.
Do you know what it is?

_____

What could it be used for?

_____
_____

How would the world be different
if this was not invented?

_____
_____
_____
_____
_____
_____
_____
_____
_____

Write down an inspirational quote:

To-Do List

Nature Study

Go outside and make a realistic drawing of something you find in in nature.

Reading Time - 1 Hour

Choose Four Books - Read from each book for 15 minutes.
Copy a sentence or picture from each book here:

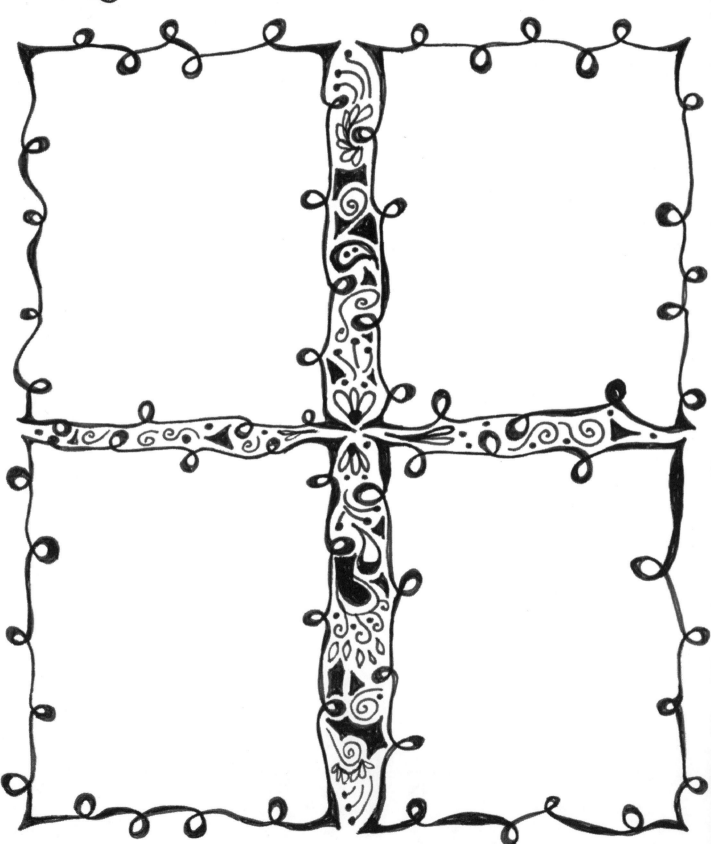

Copywork

Find an interesting paragraph in one of your books and copy it. Be diligent to make your writing look exactly like it does the book.

TITLE:_____

Page Number:_____

Emotions & Moods

How are your feeling today? Color the facial expressions to match today's moods.

Can you of three things that might help your mood improve?
1.
2.
3.

Listening Time

Listen to an audio book or classical music or ask someone to read a story to you while you color and draw on the next page.

What are you listening to?

_____

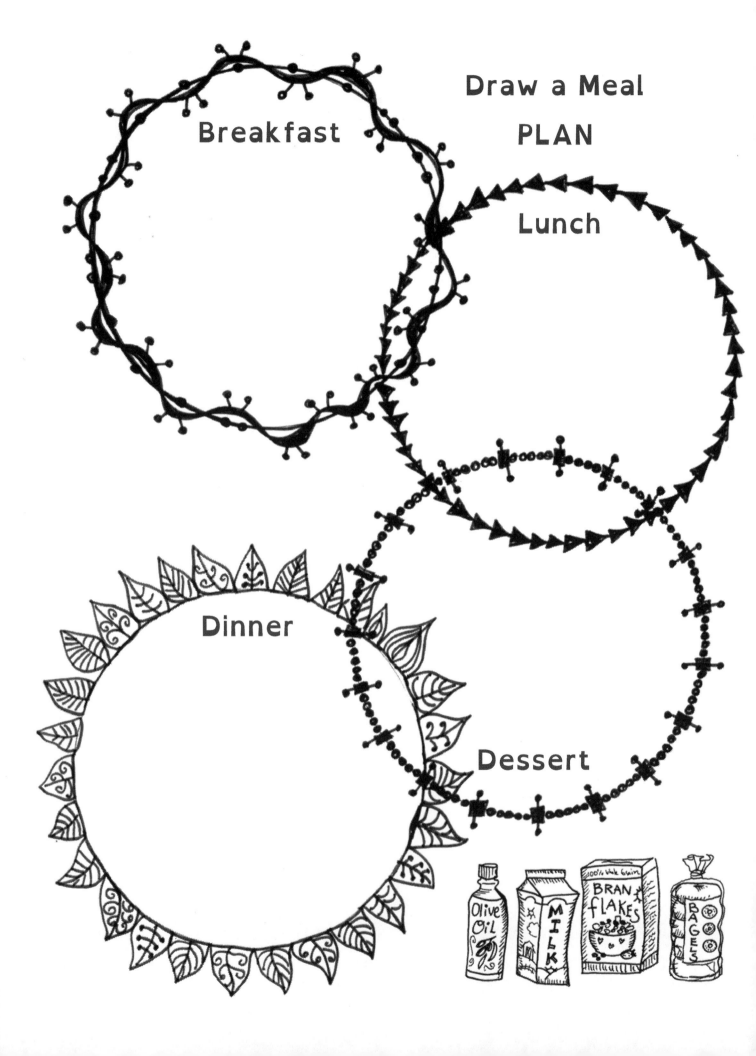

Recipe:

_____

Serves:

Prep Time:

Ingredients:

Instructions:

Shopping List:

Reading Time - 1 Hour
Choose Four Books - Read from each book for 15 minutes.
Copy a sentence or picture from each book here:

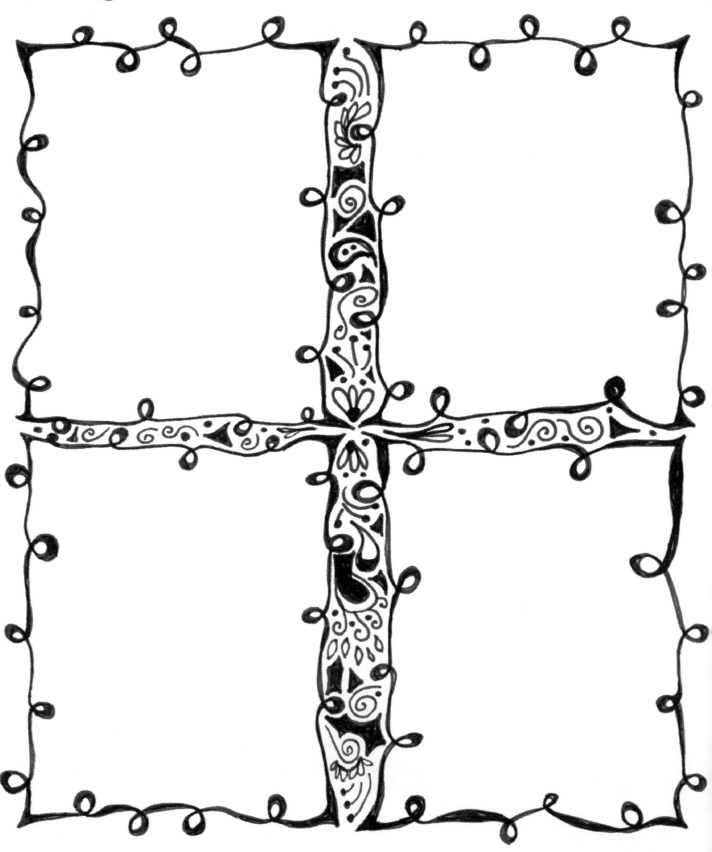

Copywork

Find an interesting paragraph in one of your books and copy it. Be diligent to make your writing look exactly like it does the book.

TITLE:_____

Page Number:_____

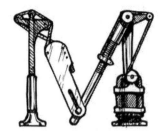

Math Practice

You can design something. You can make graphs, maps, or geometric designs. You can practice math problems.

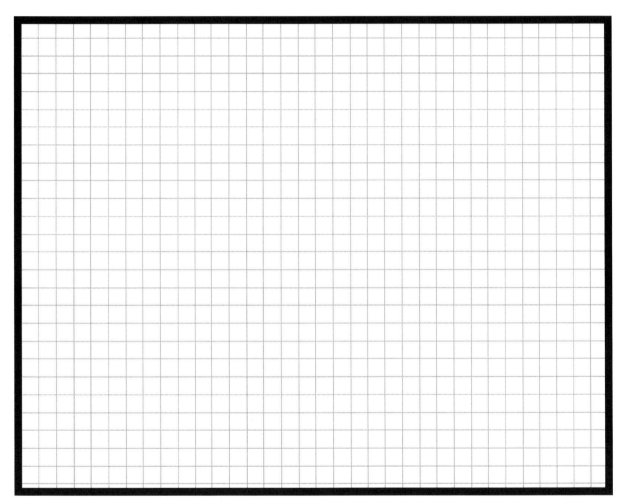

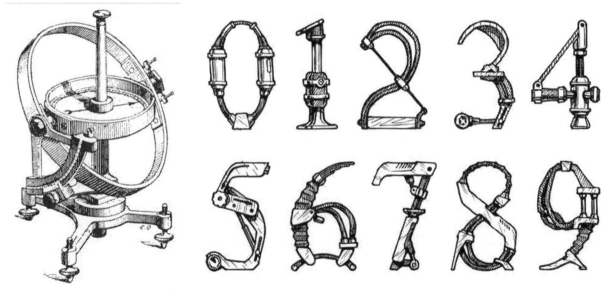

Font Writing Practice:

ABCDEFGHIJKLMNOPQURSTUVWXYZ

abcdefghijklmnopqrstuvwxyz

ABCDEFGHIJKLMNOPQURSTUVWXYZ

ABCDEFGHIJKLMNOPQURSTUVWXYZ

abcdefghijklmnopqrstuvwxyz

Object Lesson

Look at this interesting object from the past.
Do you know what it is?

_____

What could it be used for?

_____
_____

How would the world be different
if this was not invented?

_____
_____
_____
_____
_____
_____
_____
_____
_____

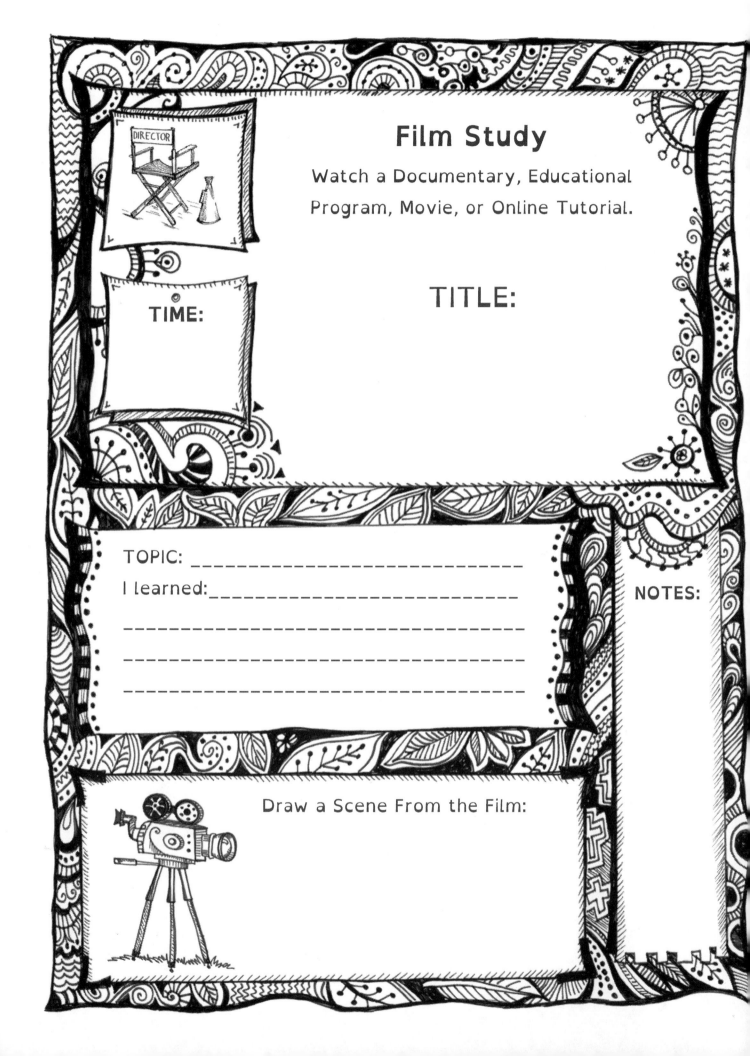

Spelling Time

Find 20 Words with 9 letters each.
Look in your books for words.
Write the words here:

Do It Yourself HOMESCHOOL JOURNALS

Copyright Information

Do It YOURSELF Homeschool Journal, and electronic printable downloads are for Home and Family use only. You may make copies of these materials for only the children in your household.

All other uses of this material must be permitted in writing by the Thinking Tree LLC. It is a violation of copyright law to distribute the electronic files or make copies for your friends, associates or students without our permission.

For information on using these materials for businesses, co-ops, summer camps, day camps, daycare, afterschool program, churches, or schools please contact us for licensing.

Contact Us:

The Thinking Tree LLC
617 N. Swope St. Greenfield, IN 46140. United States
317.622.8852 PHONE (Dial +1 outside of the USA) 267.712.7889 FAX
www.DyslexiaGames.com
jbrown@DyslexiaGames.com

Made in United States
Orlando, FL
20 September 2024

51376880R00178